The Autobiography
of
St. Margaret Mary Alacoque

" . . . thou shalt possess the treasures of My
Heart . . . and I will permit thee to distribute
them as thou wilt, in favor of souls that are
ready to receive them."
—Words of Our Lord
to St. Margaret Mary

Saint Margaret Mary Alacoque
Nun of the Order of the Visitation
of Holy Mary
1647-1690

The Autobiography
of
St. Margaret Mary Alacoque

Translation of the Authentic French Text by
The Sisters of the Visitation
Partridge Green, Horsham, West Sussex
(formerly of Roselands, Walmer, Kent)

"Thou must not keep these graces to thyself, nor be sparing in distributing them to others, for I have willed to use thy heart as a channel for conveying them into souls according to My designs; by this means many will be saved from the abyss of perdition."

—Words of Our Lord
to St. Margaret Mary

TAN BOOKS AND PUBLISHERS, INC.
Rockford, Illinois 61105

Nihil Obstat : ÆLREDUS WHITACRE, O.P.

Imprimatur : ✠ GEORGIUS AMBROSIUS, Ep. Cl.

die 30 *Iunii*, 1930.

This edition first published in 1930 by the Sisters of the Visitation, Roselands, Walmer, Kent, England. Reprinted in 1952 (as part of the Visitation Library series).

Reprinted by TAN Books and Publishers, Inc. by permission of the Sisters of the Visitation, Partridge Green.

Library of Congress Catalog Card No.: 86-50148

ISBN: 0-89555-295-7

Printed and bound in the United States of America.

TAN BOOKS AND PUBLISHERS, INC.
P.O. Box 424
Rockford, Illinois 61105

1986

"I constitute thee heiress of My Heart and of all Its treasures, for time and for eternity, allowing thee to dispose of them according to thy desire; and I promise thee that My assistance will not fail thee as long as My Heart fails not in power. Thou shalt be forever Its beloved disciple."

—*Words of Our Lord*
   to St. Margaret Mary

V ✠ J !

PREFACE
TO THE ENGLISH EDITION OF 1930

No more eloquent testimony has been or could be given
to the Saint whose complete Autobiography is here published for the first time in English, than the words of
His Holiness Pope Benedict XV on March 17th, 1918,
in the decree proclaiming that the Holy See might safely
proceed to canonization. After stating how " the
pious daughter of St. Francis of Sales received from
Jesus Himself the mission of making known the riches
of His Divine Heart that men might come to it as a
fount of grace and model of virtue," the Holy Father
adds these striking words, " the historian may say to-day
her story is completed ; the theologian and canonist have
carried their researches and examinations to the full
length ; from the hands of even the most critical the
arms have fallen . . . there can be no room for delay
in recognizing the *universal character of her apostolate*."
Then referring to the former decree of January 6th, 1918,
approving the miracles, Pope Benedict says, " the previous decree enlightened you as to the sanctity of the
devotion to the Sacred Heart ; to-day's decree should
fill you with love for it. The first decree might counsel
virtue, the last should persuade you *even to heroism* in
the practice of the devotion to the Sacred Heart of

Jesus." At the conclusion of the decree, His Holiness repeats again with an emphasis truly remarkable, " devotion to the Sacred Heart of Jesus supposes also triumph over human respect."

These passages are noteworthy because consciously or unconsciously they are in perfect harmony with the conclusions at which a prayerful reader of the *Autobiography* will arrive, viz., that the Saint is appealing to every heart and to answer the appeal will often be a call to " heroism." Read in this spirit these pages, touching in their simple obedience and humility, will not only enlighten and convince the mind but their wonderful unction will inspire the peace and confidence Our Lord Himself promises. We are in communion with a Saint; we are privileged to share her fears, her ecstasies of love, even the very weaknesses that are her true strength. All this is a great means of grace offered to whosoever will take it in the spirit of living faith. The *Autobiography* is not merely a book for spiritual reading, it is a treasure house of spiritual strength and encouragement to be read kneeling at one's prie-dieu or, better still, in the presence of that Divine Master Who deigned Himself to write its most glowing pages first on her heart as she bowed prostrate in adoration before His Eucharistic throne.

A word as to the book itself is necessary. The best history of the *Autobiography* is gathered from the depositions of Sister Claude de Farges, who was infirmarian at the Convent of Paray-le-Monial during the last illness of the Saint, given in the process of 1715. Apparently, as the Sister states, the dying religious in the midst of the consolations she experienced became alarmed at the very thought of any honour being paid to herself or her

writings after death and so she said " write, I beseech
you, dear Sister, to Father Rolin and ask him to burn
my letters and to keep inviolably the secret which I have
so often asked of him." Not content with this, a little
later she more earnestly implored the same Sister " to
burn the copybook which you will find in the cupboard
and which was written by order of my confessor, Father
Rolin of the Society of Jesus, who forbade me to destroy
it myself before he had examined it." This ' copybook '
is the *Autobiography* which is still treasured at Paray-le-
Monial as a precious relic. It measures about seven
inches by nine inches and contains sixty-four pages,
clearly and closely written by the Saint's own hand.
Father Francis Rolin, S.J., had ordered her to write this
account of Our Lord's relations with her soul. She
obeyed with great repugnance, encouraged even by her
Divine Spouse Himself it would seem, and the work
was completed in 1685. Fortunately the Father had
forbidden her to destroy the writing and happily also
the veneration of Sister de Farges for her patient caused
her to disobey the request. Indeed the good Sister per-
suaded St. Margaret Mary that it was a more perfect
act to give the key of the cupboard to the Reverend
Mother and to make a sacrifice of everything else into
the hands of God. This was promptly done " although
it cost her not a little " and the sacred manuscript was
saved.

Father Gallifet, S.J., was the first to publish it in a
treatise on the Sacred Heart which appeared in Rome
in 1726 and afterwards in 1733 in French. However,
certain liberties of style and diction were taken in these
and subsequent versions altering the authentic text. In
the translation before us the original has been most

exactly followed and praiseworthy effort has been made to preserve the simple charm of the *Vie par elle-même* published at Paray-le-Monial in 1918 and which has already passed well beyond ten thousand copies.

The Sisters of The Visitation, Walmer, have indeed merited our gratitude for making this great spiritual heirloom of their Institute accessible to all in English-speaking countries.

W. PEERS SMITH, S.J.

Feast of St. Margaret Mary 1929.

V ✠ J !

PREFACE
TO THE FRENCH EDITION OF 1924

In publishing the " Life of St. Margaret Mary written by herself " in a separate volume we knew well that we were complying with the wishes of a limited few, but we did not think that these few would so quickly be transformed into an ever-increasing multitude. However, such is the charm which the very humble pages of the great Saint of Paray work in souls that thousands of copies of her *Autobiography* have been circulated in a very short time. It is for us to make provision that they can always be procured, and for this reason we are now publishing a new edition, smaller in size than the preceding—to meet the demands expressed on this subject. Henceforth the authentic text may be more easily meditated.

The more a portrait resembles the original, the greater value it has. Now, in her *Autobiography*, not only does Saint Margaret Mary narrate her life with perfect simplicity and sincerity, but she describes herself such as she was and such as she saw herself by the light of the Holy Ghost. This last phrase is very important, and must never be lost sight of, lest one be tempted to accuse the Saint of exaggeration and of want of moderation in her appreciation of herself. When the divine light penetrates the souls of saints, it sheds such clear rays that they discover what they call " big sins," where we can only see the smallest imperfections, or simple faults of human weakness. For example, we hear, on the one hand, Saint Margaret Mary saying and repeating that she had " committed great crimes," that she " offended her God so much," while, on the other hand, her confessors affirm that she had preserved her baptismal innocence.[1] In this difference of opinion, which side is to be believed ? We dare reply : " Both ! "

It is indeed certain that the Saint never gravely offended Our Lord, for she had never lost her baptismal innocence: the judgment of her directors bears witness to this. But she herself, Margaret Mary—the Confidante of the Heart of Jesus—accustomed to live in the presence of the " Sanctity of love and of justice," sees such a distance between the relative purity of her soul and the absolute purity of the God Whom she loves, that she stigmatizes as imperfection and sin all that is not in accordance with this Divine Purity. Hence she is almost continually bemoaning the offences and the ingratitude of which she believes herself guilty towards God. . . . Hence, too, that habitual state of confusion in presence of her own unworthiness in which we see her plunged. Must we take offence at all this or be astonished ? By no means ! She is the privileged disciple instructed directly by the Lord of Lords who has said to her : " Learn that I am a holy Master, and One Who teaches holiness. I am pure and cannot endure the slightest stain." Therefore the Saint of Paray is right in deploring her slightest faults so bitterly, and one of the beauties of her *Autobiography* is that it shows us to what degree Divine Love is

[1] Cp. Circular of the Monastery of Paray, August 8th, 1691, and the work of Father Croiset, edition 1691.

capable of inciting humility in a heart It has completely captivated.

Moreover, there is no anxiety whatever as to form in all this narrative written by obedience. In the opinion of the esteemed Mgr. Gauthey, these are " admirable pages " in which sublime matter and words are inserted without the least affectation.[1] We here behold a soul possessed by no other hunger and thirst than that of glorifying her Sovereign Lord Who has chosen her for such great designs, without her ever feeling self-complacency because of this Divine choice. When once a movement of vanity attempts to rise in the inferior part of her soul, instantly the Voice of the heavenly Master restores order by this severe reprimand : " What hast thou, dust and ashes, in which thou canst glory ? " And our Saint again sinks back into her nothingness.

Several times she had received the order to write what was passing within her. As this seemed to her beyond her power, she had been ingenious in seeking means to reconcile her submission to the command given with her horror of speaking of herself, destroying what she had first written, and so hoping there would be no mention of her, either during her life or after her death. But her director, Father F. J. Rolin, S.J., who had been a first time in Paray from 1683–1684 and had been absent from 1684–1685 in order to make his third year of probation, returned thither in 1685. It was then that he enjoined upon St. Margaret Mary to write her life, giving her the order that she was not to burn anything herself before he had examined it. She began forthwith, confessing, in the very first lines, that it was God alone Who knew the extent of the repugnance " she felt in so doing."

[1] *Life and works*, Vol. II, page 24.

The R. P. Rolin left Paray in the autumn of 1686, before having been able to peruse the Memoir, which thus remained unfinished, for the Saint ceased writing after the Father's departure. When she felt herself dying, she trembled at the thought of leaving the manuscript behind her, and begged Sister Péronne-Rosalie de Farges to burn it, as she had been forbidden to do so herself. Sister de Farges took good care not to comply with her request. She simply induced the dying Sister to give up to the Superior[1] the key of the cupboard which contained the writing, and offer to God on this occasion the sacrifice of her own will. Margaret Mary did so, though it cost her much.

Such was the way in which Providence provided that this most important document should be preserved to posterity as exceptional evidence, not only of the holiness of this chosen soul, but still more of the truth of the Revelations of the Sacred Heart.

Kept in the Monastery of the Visitation of Paray-le-Monial as a treasured relic, this manuscript is 146 millimetres wide and 200 long, comprising 64 pages, very compact and filled with that beautiful and characteristic writing which still charms those who read it. This autograph was certified as true by Sister Anne-Elizabeth de la Garde and signed by Dom de Bansière at the Process of July 22nd, 1715.

Father de Gallifet, Assistant of France to the Very Rev. Father General of the Society of Jesus, obtained from Sister de la Garde an authentic copy of this precious Memoir. On March 6th, 1725, he thanks the Superior of Paray in these words : "A few days ago I received the ' Life of the Ven. Sister Margaret

[1] Mother Catherine-Antoinette de Lévy-Châteaumorand.

Alacoque.' The boat in which the ' Life ' and the other packets were sent us from Marseilles was wrecked near Livourne. The packets remained four days in the water, but were recovered. The copybook in which the ' Life ' is written was unspoilt, and it reached me in almost as good a condition as if nothing had happened to it. I hope to receive great assistance from the reading of this Memoir for the Glory of the Sacred Heart of Jesus Christ."

Father de Gallifet was the first to make it known in his Latin book on the Sacred Heart, a work which was published in Rome at the end of 1726. When he returned to France, one of his first cares was to translate his Latin book into French, and the first edition appeared in 1733. Several others followed. That of 1743 contained not only the ' Mémoire de la Sœur Marguerite ' —but also Father de Gallifet's Apologetic Preface on the Saint's Memoir.

Father de Gallifet, when publishing the *Life of the Servant of God* written by herself, attempted to improve the style, following thereby the customs and tastes of the period, but in so doing he deprived it of some of its original charm. It was still the account of the same marvellous graces, but was no longer told, in any respect, after the manner of her who had been their recipient. When in 1867 the Visitation of Paray published a first edition of the *Oeuvres de la Bienheureuse*, it was considered desirable to restore the original text of the *Vie par elle-même*. Nevertheless it had been thought necessary to suppress certain passages, to omit certain words, and, on the contrary, to add others in brackets, so as to make the " reading more fluent." As this method is no longer used nowadays, we are giving purely and simply the text of the Saint, just as she wrote it herself. Doubtless, and we are far from denying it, there are faulty sentences, some are too long, others incomplete or obscure. But what does it matter ? Let us note well and remember, it is not a literary work which the Saint composes, but it is the simple account of the incessant and prodigious graces with which she was favoured that she writes down under the eye of God alone. The less she has studied the manner of writing this account, the more impressive has she rendered it, freeing it thereby from all human admixture. Let us add that, when we think of the number of times she had to recommence writing this Memoir, and very probably without ever reading it over—Our Lord not allowing it—we wonder rather that there are not more mistakes.

We have retained the 111 marginal notes so opportunely introduced by Mgr. Gauthey in regard to the text, which facilitate all research. We have only added here and there some footnotes to help the reader to find his way in this story where the Saint mentions no names, and observes no chronological order. We have, of course, used modern spelling, except that we have often, according to the custom of the times, left the verb and adjective, occurring after several subjects, in the singular number. The words in brackets are only to supply those wanting in the original, they are necessary to make the text intelligible.

The Divine Master had promised His faithful servant to shed the unction of His grace over all she wrote through pure obedience. May He deign to fulfil this promise in favour of all who read the following pages, and may all learn therefrom how to sanctify themselves in the school of the Sacred Heart of Jesus and of Saint Margaret Mary.

Her Cause has gloriously triumphed over every obstacle, and Providence has wished that, after all the horrors of the Great War, her Canonization should be preceded by the splendour of the Consecration of the Basilica of the " Vœu National " on the hill of Montmartre, as though to prove, not only to France but to the whole world, that Margaret Mary had really accomplished her mission, and that this faithful Messenger of God's love to men was worthy of being inscribed in the Catalogue of Saints. *Exaltavit humiles !* Such is indeed the sublime lesson to be drawn from the humble life and the magnificent exaltation of Margaret Mary in the very brilliance of the reign of the Sacred Heart. More than ever, since her Canonization, has the Saint been faithful to her mission of extending this blessed reign over the whole world, and how does she accomplish this ? She turns souls towards the Sacred Heart, she leads them to It and draws down upon each the graces of salvation and of sanctification of which It is the source. And thus by the Will of God, St. Margaret Mary is a channel of mercy in the Church. In the first of the great Apparitions, did not Our Lord say to His beloved disciple : " My Divine Heart is so inflamed with love for all mankind, and for thee in particular, that, being no longer able to contain within Itself the flames of this ardent charity, they must be spread abroad through thy means " ? And this is being realized each day more and more. How can we witness it without returning thanks to God ?

From our Monastery of Paray-le-Monial,

March 25th, 1924.

D. S. B.

*cest du profond abime de mon neant que
ie me prosterne devant vs o tres sacre
divin et adorable cr de Jesus pr vous
randre tout les homages d'amour de
louange & d'adoration dont ie suis
capable*

(From the depth of my nothingness, I prostrate myself before Thee,
O Most Sacred, Divine and Adorable Heart of Jesus, to pay Thee
all the homage of love, praise and adoration in my power.)

LIFE

OF

SAINT MARGARET MARY ALACOQUE

WRITTEN BY HERSELF

———

V ✠ J!

IT is for the love of Thee, O my God, and through obedience, that I submit to write this account, asking
Thy pardon for the resistance I have made. Thou alone knowest how great my repugnance thereto is; Thou alone therefore canst give me strength to overcome it, for this obedience was given me by Thee, in order to punish the exceeding pleasure which I have ever felt and the precaution I had taken to bury myself in entire oblivion on the part of creatures. It was after having obtained a promise from persons who I thought would be able to help me in this, and after I had committed to the flames what remained to me of the former account I had written through obedience, that this present order was given me. Grant, O my Sovereign Good, that I may write nothing but what may be for Thy greater glory and my own confusion.

1. The Saint undertakes to write this account through obedience.

O my only Love! how much I am indebted to Thee!
. . . From my tenderest years Thou didst prevent me
with Thy grace and didst constitute
2. Her horror of Thyself the Master and possessor of my
sin. Vow of heart, although Thou knewest full well
Chastity. the resistance it would make Thee. As
soon as I was able to know myself,
Thou didst manifest to my soul the hideousness of sin,
the sight of which imprinted in my heart so intense a
horror thereof, that the least stain was an insupportable
torment to me. In order to check my childish vivacity,
it sufficed to say that God would be offended; this
would make me stop at once and turn away from what
I wanted to do.

Without knowing their meaning, I felt continually
urged to pronounce the following words: " O my God,
I consecrate to Thee my purity, and I make Thee a vow
of perpetual chastity." This I did once between the
two elevations at Mass which I was wont to hear on my
bare knees, even in the coldest weather. I did not then
understand what I had done, nor what was meant by
the words " vow " and " chastity," but my sole desire
was to hide myself in some wood, and the only thing
that prevented me from doing so was the fear of meeting
with men.

The Blessed Virgin has always taken great care of me.
I had recourse to her in all my necessities, and she has
preserved me from great dangers. I
3. Protection of did not dare address myself to her
the Blessed divine Son, but only to her, and I often
Virgin. presented her with the little crown of
the rosary, which I said on my bare knees, or genuflec-
ting and kissing the ground at every Ave Maria.

I lost my father when I was very young, and my mother having taken upon herself the guardianship of her five

4. Death of her father, 1655. children, was seldom at home ; being the only daughter,[1] I was left until the age of eight and a half without any other education than that which I received from the servants and from the people of the village.

I was then sent to a Convent, where I made my First Communion when about nine years of age. This

5. She is placed in the school of the Urbanist nuns at Charolles, where she makes her First Communion. Communion shed such bitterness over all my little pleasures and amusements that I was no longer able to enjoy any of them, although I sought them eagerly. Whenever I wanted to join in the games of my companions, I always

felt something which called me and drew me aside into some little corner, leaving me no peace until I had followed it. Our Lord then made me give myself to prayer, and I did so almost always either prostrate or on my bare knees or making genuflections, provided nobody saw me, for it was a strange torment to me when I was noticed.

I also felt a great desire to do everything that I saw the nuns do, for I looked upon them all as saints and thought that, if I were a religious, I, too, should become one like them. This filled me with so great a longing (for the religious state) that I thought of nothing else, although, for my part, I did not consider the nuns sufficiently secluded ; but, not knowing any others, I imagined I ought to remain with them.

I fell, however, into so pitiable a state of ill-health that for about four years I was unable to walk, my bones

[1] Her younger sister Gilberte, born 1649, had died in 1655.

piercing my skin. Consequently I was removed from the Convent at the end of two years ; but, as no remedy could be found for my illness, I was consecrated to the Blessed Virgin, with the promise that, if she cured me, I should one day be one of her daughters. Scarcely had I made this vow, than I was cured and taken anew under the protection of Our Lady. She made herself so completely Mistress of my heart, that, looking upon me as her own, she governed me as wholly dedicated to her, reproving me for my faults and teaching me how to do the Will of God. It happened once that, being seated while reciting the rosary, she appeared to me and gave me the following reprimand which, although very young at the time, I have never forgotten : " I am surprised, my daughter," she said, " that you serve me so negligently ! " These words left such an impression on my soul, that they have served me for my whole life.

6. Her long illness. She is cured by the Blessed Virgin.

On recovering my health, I thought only of seeking pleasure in the enjoyment of my liberty, without concerning myself much about the fulfilment of my promise. But, O my God, I little thought then, what later on Thou didst give me to understand and experience, namely, that, the Sacred Heart having brought me forth on Calvary with so much sorrow, the life which Thou didst then give me could be fed and maintained only by the Cross, and, therefore, this would be my most delightful food. Thus, as soon as I had recovered, I gave myself up to vanity and the affection of creatures, flattering myself that the tenderness which my mother and brothers had for me would allow me to amuse and enjoy myself as

7. She gives way to dissipation.

much as I liked. But Thou, O my God, didst make me see that I was out in my reckoning, which had been made according to my inclinations naturally drawn to pleasure, and not according to Thy designs which were very different from mine.

My mother having despoiled herself of all authority in her house, those into whose hands she had given it,

8. Domestic Persecution. exercised it in such a manner that both she and I were reduced to a state of captivity; but I do not wish to blame those persons by what I am about to say, nor do I think that they did wrong in causing me to suffer. My God did not permit me to have this thought, but wished that I should regard them as instruments employed by Him for the accomplishment of His Holy Will. We therefore had no longer any power in the house and dared not do anything without permission. It was a continual battle; everything was kept under lock and key, so much so that I was often unable to find anything to put on in order to go to Mass, and was even obliged to borrow both hat and coat. It was at such times especially that I began to realize my captivity, to which, however, I submitted myself so completely that I never did the least thing, nor did I leave the house, without the consent of these three persons.[1]

From that time all my affections turned towards the Blessed Sacrament of the Altar, where I sought my only delight and consolation. But being in a village and at

---

[1] These three persons, whom in her perfect spirit of charity St. Margaret Mary is careful not to name, were : 1st, her grandmother, Jeanne Delaroche, widow of Claude Alacoque ; 2nd, her aunt, Benoîte Alacoque, wife of Toussaint Delaroche ; 3rd, her great-aunt, Benoîte de Meulin, widow of Simon Delaroche and mother of Toussaint. She sometimes went by the name of " Mother Chappendye," from the name of her native village.

some distance from the church, I could go there only with the consent of the above-mentioned persons, and it so happened that, when one was willing, another was not. Often when I showed my grief by tears, they reproached me with having made an appointment with some young men, saying that I was disappointed at not being able to meet them and be flattered and made much of; and that the desire to go to Mass or Benediction of the Blessed Sacrament was only a pretext I gave. Yet I had such a horror in my heart for anything of the kind that I would rather have consented to see my body torn into a thousand pieces than entertain such a thought. At such times I knew not where to take refuge, except in some corner of the garden or stable or other secluded place, where I could kneel and pour out my heart in tears before God through the medium of the Blessed Virgin, my good Mother, in whom I had placed all my confidence. There I remained whole days without food or drink, and as this occurred frequently, poor people of the village sometimes had pity on me and, towards evening, gave me a little milk or fruit. On returning to the house afterwards, it was with such fear and trembling that I seemed to myself like a poor criminal about to receive her sentence of condemnation. I should have considered myself happier to beg my bread than live in this manner, for many a time I dared not take any food when at table. The moment I entered the house, the battle began worse than ever, because I had not attended to the house and to the children of those dear benefactresses of my soul, and, without being permitted to utter a word, I set myself to work with the servants.

I spent the nights as I had spent the days, shedding

tears at the foot of my crucifix. There I was given to see, without my understanding it, that He desired to be the absolute Master of my heart and render me conformable in all things to His suffering life. That was why He wished to constitute Himself my Master, making my soul feel His presence, in order to enable me to act as He did in the midst of His cruel sufferings, which He had borne for love of me.

My soul was henceforth so penetrated with this thought that I would not have wished my sufferings to cease for a moment. For from that time He was always present to me under the form of the crucifix or of an *Ecce Homo*, or as carrying His cross. This filled me with such feelings of compassion and so great a love of suffering that whatever I had to bear seemed but light in comparison with the ardent desire I had to suffer, that thereby I might render myself conformable to my suffering Jesus. I was sorry when those hands, which at times were raised to strike me, were stayed from venting upon me all their rigour. I felt continually urged to render all kinds of services to those true friends of my soul and would willingly have sacrificed myself for them; it was my greatest pleasure to do good to them and speak as well as possible of them. But it was not I who did all that I now write and shall hereafter relate, much against my will. It was my Sovereign Master, Who, having taken possession of my will, did not permit me to utter any complaint, to murmur or to bear any resentment against those persons; nor would He allow anyone to show me pity or compassion, saying that He Himself had been thus treated, and He willed that, when I could not prevent people speaking to me about them, I should excuse them

9. Ecce Homo. Love of suffering.

and take the blame for myself, adding, what is indeed
true, that my sins deserved much more.

I have always taken every care and precaution to conceal all that I am now writing, so that naught might be
known hereafter, even endeavouring
not to retain any remembrance of it, in
order to leave all to the memory of
my Good Master. I therefore complained to Him of the great repugnance that I felt, but He said to me :
" Continue, My daughter, continue, neither more nor
less will come of all this repugnance ; My Will must
be accomplished."—" But alas ! my God, how can I
remember what happened more than twenty-five years
ago ? "—" Dost thou not know that I am the eternal
memory of My Heavenly Father, by Whom nothing is
forgotten, and before Whom the past and the future are
as the present ? Write, therefore, without fear, according as I shall dictate to thee, and I promise thee the
unction of My grace in order that I may be thereby
glorified.

" In the first place I desire this of thee, in order to
show thee that I baffle and render useless all the pre-
cautions which I have allowed thee to take, to hide the
profusion of graces with which I have taken pleasure
in enriching so poor and miserable a creature as
thyself. Thou shouldst never lose sight thereof, so
that thou mayest render Me continual thanks for
them.

" Secondly, it is to teach thee that thou must in no
way appropriate them to thyself, nor be reserved in
distributing them to others, since I desire to make use
of thy heart as of a channel through which to pour these

10. Repugnance to write her Life. Our Lord obliges her thereto and gives His reasons.

graces into souls according to My designs, by this means drawing many from the abyss of perdition, as I will show thee hereafter.

" Thirdly, it is to manifest that I am the eternal Truth, and that the graces which I have bestowed on thee are open to every kind of examination and test." After these words I felt so strengthened that, despite the great fear I have lest this account should be seen, I am resolved to continue at any cost, in order to accomplish the Will of my Sovereign Master.

The heaviest of my crosses was that of not being able to alleviate those of my mother which were a hundred times harder to bear than my own. I did not, however, give her the consolation of speaking about them for fear of offending God by the satisfaction we might have had in conversing about our troubles. I felt this most keenly when she was ill, because, being wholly abandoned to my care and attendance, she had much to suffer on this account. At times, everything was locked up, and I had even to go and beg for eggs and other things necessary for sick people. It was no little torture for my natural timidity to be thus obliged to apply to the villagers, who frequently said more to me on the subject than I would have wished. Once when she was suffering from a dangerous attack of erysipelas in the head, which was much swollen and excessively inflamed, they contented themselves with having her bled by a common village surgeon who happened to be passing by. He told me that she could not recover without a miracle, still no one showed the least trouble or concern except myself. In truth, I knew not to whom to have recourse, except to my usual refuge, the most Holy Virgin, and to my

11. Her mother's illness.

Sovereign Master[1] [to Whom alone I could confide] the anguish in which I was continually plunged. In the midst of all this, I received from those around me only contempt, injuries and accusations, and I knew not where to take refuge. On the feast of the Circumcision of Our Lord I went to Mass, and I asked Him to be Himself the Physician and remedy for my poor mother, and to teach me what I must do for her. This He did in so merciful a manner that on my return home I found the swelling had burst, leaving an open wound in the cheek, about the size of the palm of the hand, which exhaled so insupportable an odour that no one would approach her. I did not know how to dress a wound, and until then had never been able even to look at or touch one. Having no other ointment but that of Divine Providence, all I could do was to remove each day a quantity of putrid flesh, but I felt such courage and confidence in the goodness of my Sovereign Who seemed to be always present, that, in a few days, contrary to all expectation, the wound was healed.

During the time of her illness, I seldom went to bed or slept ; I scarcely took any food, and often passed entire days without eating. But my Divine Master consoled and strengthened me with perfect conformity to His most holy Will, so that I had recourse to Him in all that happened to me, saying : " O my Sovereign Master ! this would not have happened if Thou hadst not willed it so, but I return Thee thanks for having permitted it, that thereby I may be made more like unto Thee."

[1] The words in brackets, being torn in the MS., we have supplied them from the text by the contemporaries which is probably conformable to the original.

In the midst of all this, I felt strongly drawn to mental prayer, and this likewise was a cause of much suffering to me, as I knew not how to make it, nor how to learn to do so, not having any opportunity of conversing with spiritual persons ; all I knew of it was the single word 'mental prayer,' by which my heart was ravished. I again addressed myself to my Sovereign Master, and He taught me the manner in which He wished me to make it, which has served me for my whole life. He made me prostrate myself humbly before Him to ask His pardon for everything by which I had offended Him, and, after an act of adoration, I offered Him my prayer, without knowing how to set about it.

12. Her attraction for mental prayer.

He then presented Himself to me in the mystery in which He desired me to consider Him, applied my mind so closely to it, and kept my soul and all my powers so absorbed in Him that I felt no distraction. My heart was consumed with the desire of loving Him, which gave me an insatiable longing for Holy Communion and for suffering. However, I knew not what to do, for I had no time at my disposal except the night, of which I spent as much as I could in prayer. But although this occupation was inexpressibly delightful to me, I did not think it was a form of prayer, and, feeling myself ceaselessly urged to pray, I promised my Divine Master that, as soon as He had taught it to me, I would give to it all the time I could. Nevertheless, His Goodness kept me so strongly occupied in the manner I have just said that it gave me a distaste for vocal prayers, which I could never say when in presence of the Blessed Sacrament, being then so absorbed in prayer that I never felt weary.

I could have passed whole days and nights there, without eating or drinking, and without knowing what I was doing, except that I was being consumed in His presence like a burning taper, in order to return Him love for love. I could not remain at the entrance of the church and, inspite of the confusion I felt, I never failed to go as near as I could to the Blessed Sacrament. I envied and counted those alone happy who were able to communicate often and who were at liberty to remain before the most Holy Sacrament, although it is true that I made bad use of my time, and I fear that I did nothing but dishonour It. I also strove to gain the good will of the persons of whom I have spoken above, that I might thus obtain some moments before the Blessed Sacrament. It happened once that, before Christmas, the parish priest gave out from the pulpit that whoever should not have slept on Christmas Eve could not go to Communion; as in punishment for my sins I was never able to sleep on the vigil of Christmas, I did not dare communicate.[1] That day of rejoicing was consequently for me a day of tears which took the place of food and pleasure.

13. Her love for the Blessed Sacrament and her desire for Holy Communion.

I had indeed committed great crimes, for once during the days of Carnival, together with other young girls, I disguised myself through vain complacency. This has been to me a cause of bitter tears and sorrow during my whole life, together with the fault I committed in adorning myself in worldly attire through the same

14. Her greatest fault.

---

[1] The strange but popular belief that one must have slept before approaching the Holy Table on Christmas night was at that time more or less general, and evidently M. Antoine Alacoque, Curé of Verosvres, shared it.

motive of complacency towards the persons above mentioned. They were, however, employed by God as instruments of Divine Justice to avenge Himself for the injuries I had done Him by my sins, for they were virtuous persons and had no bad intention in acting as they did with regard to us, and I truly believe that they failed not in any way, since it was my God Who willed it thus, and I felt no ill-will towards them.

Alas! my Lord, have pity upon my weakness in the excess of grief and confusion which, while writing this,

15. Her confusion at having to write this account. Thou dost make me feel so vividly owing to the long resistance I have made Thee. Sustain me, O my God, that I may not succumb under the rigour of these just reproaches. No, I protest that, with the help of Thy grace, I will never more resist Thee, even though it should cost me my life and draw upon me the contempt of creatures; yea, though all the fury of hell should rise up in arms against me to avenge Thee. I implore Thy pardon for my resistance, and I beseech Thee to grant me the strength to accomplish what Thou desirest of me, in spite of the repugnance which my self-love makes me feel.

But to continue: as I grew up, my crosses increased; for the devil, in order to make me fail against the vow I

16. She is sought in marriage. had made, brought about that I should be presented with several advantageous offers of marriage. This drew to the house much company that I was obliged to see, and this was no little torture to me. For, on the one hand, my relations pressed me to accept; and my mother, incessantly weeping, told me that she looked to me as her only hope of putting an end to her misery by joining me as soon as I should be settled in the world, adding that this would be a great consolation to her.—On the other hand, God pursued my heart so powerfully that I had no longer any peace, for not only was my vow constantly before my eyes, but I also thought of the fearful torments which awaited me, if I should fail to keep it. The devil especially took advantage of the tender affection which I had for my mother, unceasingly representing to me the tears she shed, suggesting that she would die of grief if I became a nun and that, as she depended entirely upon me for the care and attendance she required, I would be responsible for her death before God. This was an unbearable torment to me, because we loved each other so dearly that we could not bear to be parted. Thus the desire to be a nun, and the extreme horror I had of anything against purity haunted me without ceasing.

All this made me suffer a martyrdom, for I had no respite, and many were the tears I shed, not knowing what course to take and having no one to whom I could open my heart. Finally, the tender love for my mother began to get the upper hand, and I thought that, as I was but a child when I made my vow and did not understand the meaning thereof, I could easily obtain a dispensation from it. Added to this I dreaded renouncing my liberty, for I thought I should no longer be able to fast, give alms and take the discipline as often as I wished; and also that the religious life required such great holiness in those who embraced it, that it would be impossible for me ever to attain to it, and that I should lose my soul in the cloister.

I therefore began to frequent society and to adorn myself in order to please others, trying to enjoy myself

as much as I could.   Thou, O my God, wert the sole
witness of the extent and duration of this terrible interior

conflict, to which I should have suc-
17.   The world   cumbed a thousand times over, had it
attracts her.   In-   not been for the special help of Thy
terior conflict.   merciful Goodness, which had designs
over me far other than those I planned in my heart.   On
this occasion, as on many others, Thou didst give me to
understand that it would be hard and difficult to resist the
powerful goad of Thy love.   And, although in my malice
and infidelity I employed all my strength and made use
of every device to oppose it and stifle its every movement
in me, all was in vain, for in the midst of company and
amusement it aimed such burning darts at my heart that
they pierced and consumed it on all sides ; and the pain
I felt in consequence rendered me quite speechless.

This not being enough to cause a heart so ungrateful
as mine to yield, I felt myself bound, as it were, with
cords and dragged with such force that I was at last
constrained to follow Him Who called me.   He then
led me to some secluded place, where He reproved me
severely, for He was jealous of my miserable heart, a
prey to such untold persecution.   Prostrating myself
with my face to the ground, I asked His pardon, and He
then made me take a long and severe discipline.   Nevertheless, in spite of all this, I recommenced my resistance
as before and returned to my vanities.   But when, at
night, I took off those accursed liveries of Satan, namely
all that worldly attire, the instrument of his malice, my
Sovereign Master presented Himself to me torn and
disfigured as at the time of His scourging, and with
bitter reproaches He said that it was my vanity which
had reduced Him to that state, and that I was wasting

most precious time of which He would demand a rigorous account from me at the hour of my death. He added that I betrayed and persecuted Him, regardless of the many proofs He had given me of His love and of His desire that I should render myself conformable to Him. This made such a deep impression upon me and caused such painful wounds in my heart that I wept bitterly, and it would be difficult for me to express all that I suffered or what passed within me.

As I had never been instructed in the spiritual life nor heard anyone speak of it, I knew nothing thereof beyond what I had been taught by my Divine Master and was by Him lovingly constrained to do. In order to some extent to be avenged on myself for the injuries I did Him, and to form afresh this resemblance and conformity with Him, relieving thereby the pain which I endured, I bound this miserable and criminal body with knotted cords, which I drew so tightly that I had difficulty in breathing and eating. I left these cords so long that they were buried in the flesh which grew over them, and I could not extract them without great violence and excessive pain. I did the same with little chains which I fastened round my arms and which, on being taken off, tore away pieces of the flesh. I also slept on a plank or on sharply notched sticks, on which I took my night's rest; besides all this I took the discipline. I tried to find in these penances some relief to that severe interior struggle and pain which I felt, compared to which all that I suffered outwardly appeared as nothing—although the humiliations and contradictions were, as I said above, continually increasing rather than decreasing—all this, I repeat, seemed to be an alleviation in comparison with

18. Corporal penances.

my interior anguish. I had to do extreme violence to myself, in order to bear them in silence, according to the instructions of my Good Master, and to keep them hidden, so that nothing appeared outwardly, except that I was seen to grow pale and waste away.

The fear that I had of offending God was a greater torment to me than all the rest, for it seemed to me that my sins were continual, and they appeared to me so great that I was surprised that hell did not open under my feet to bury alive so miserable a sinner. I was seldom able to go to Confession, although I would have wished to do so every day. I looked upon those who remained long at Confession as saints, and thought they were very different from me, who knew not how to accuse myself of my faults. This made me cry bitterly.

After several years had thus passed in the midst of conflicts and various kinds of suffering, during which the only consolation I received was **19. Her desire for religious life.** that given me by my Lord Jesus Christ, Who had made Himself my Master and my Ruler, I felt the desire of the religious life rekindle itself in my heart with such intensity that I resolved to embrace it at any cost. But alas ! this could not be accomplished until four or five years later. In the meantime my conflicts and difficulties redoubled on all sides, whereas I tried to increase my penances according as my Divine Master permitted.

He now changed His manner towards me, making me see the beauty of virtue, especially of the three vows of Poverty, Chastity and Obedience and telling me that " by observing them one becomes holy " ; this He said, because, when in prayer, I often begged Him to make me a saint. I read scarcely any other books but the

Lives of the Saints, and, on opening a book, I used to
say to myself : I must find one that is easy to imitate,
so that I can do as she did in order to become a saint,
such as she was. But I was distressed to see how much
I offended my God, and thought the Saints had not
offended Him as I had, or, at least, if any of them had
done so, they had never ceased doing penance for it.
This animated me with a great desire to do likewise,
but as my Divine Master inspired me with a great fear of
following my own will, I believed even then that nothing
would be pleasing to Him, unless I did it from a motive
of love and from obedience. My heart yearned, therefore, to love Him and to perform all my actions through
obedience, though, as I knew not how to practise either
the one or the other, I thought it was a sin to say that I
loved, because it seemed to me that my actions contra-
dicted my words.

I therefore asked Him to teach me and to show me
what He wished me to do in order to please Him. This
He did in the following manner : He
20. Her charity towards the poor and infirm. inspired me with so tender a love for
the poor that I would gladly have con-
versed with no other persons. He also
impressed upon me such deep feelings of compassion
for their miseries that, had it been in my power, I would
have retained nothing for myself ; therefore when I had
any money, I gave it to poor children to induce them to
come to me, that I might teach them their Catechism and
their prayers. The consequence was that they flocked
round me in such numbers that I knew not where to
assemble them in winter except in a large room, from
which we were sometimes driven out. This was a source
of great mortification to me, for I did not wish anyone

to know what I was about. It was generally thought that I gave to the poor everything I could find, but I would not have dared do that for fear of taking what did not belong to me; I was careful to give only what was my own, and even that I did not dare do without leave. Indeed, I was obliged to use endearing words to induce my mother to allow me to give away what I had, but, as she loved me tenderly, she consented more or less willingly. If at times she refused, I remained in peace, and a little later I returned to the charge, for I could no longer do anything without permission. It was, however, not only to my mother that I subjected myself, but also to the three persons with whom we lived, which was a continual martyrdom to me. I thought I had to submit to all for whom I felt the most aversion and to obey them, in order to try whether I could be a religious. The permissions which I was continually asking drew upon me many contemptuous rebuffs and increased my captivity, for it gave them so much authority over me, that it would be impossible for a religious to be more subjected. But my ardent desire to love God enabled me to overcome all difficulties, and I was, therefore, careful to do whatever was most contrary to my inclinations and for which I felt the greatest repugnance. I was so strongly urged to this that I accused myself in confession whenever I failed to follow this impulse.

I had an extreme repugnance to look at wounds; so, in order to overcome myself, I wished to begin by kissing and dressing them, though I did not know how to set about it. But my Divine Master knew so well how to supply for my ignorance, that in a very short time, although very malignant, they were cured without other ointment than that of His Providence ; for I trusted more in His goodness than in external remedies.

I was also naturally drawn to the love of pleasure and amusement, but I no longer enjoyed them, although I sought them eagerly. The painful sight of my Saviour after the scourging hindered me from delighting in them, and the following words, with which He reproached me, pierced me to the heart :

21. Our Lord reproaches her and begins to reveal His designs in her regard.

" Wouldst thou take this pleasure, whereas I never had any and delivered Myself up to every kind of bitterness for love of thee and to win thy heart ? Nevertheless, thou wouldst still dispute it with Me." This made a deep impression on me, but I sincerely acknowledge that I understood nothing of all this, so great was my ignorance, and so little was I versed in spiritual things, and if I did any good, it was simply because He urged me so powerfully thereto that I was unable to resist. I am covered with confusion as I write all this, and I would wish it to be known how deserving I am of the most rigorous eternal chastisement on account of my continual resistance to God and my opposition to His grace. I would wish also to make known the greatness of His mercies, for it seemed as though He had undertaken constantly to pursue me and oppose His goodness to my malice, and His love to my ingratitude. The thought of my not having known how to recognize my Sovereign Redeemer, Who from my infancy had ever taken such loving care of me, has been a cause of grief to me all my life.

When I was overwhelmed with amazement on seeing that He was not repulsed by so many falls and infidelities which I beheld in myself, He gave me this answer : " It is because I desire to make of thee, as it were, a compound of My Love and of My Mercy." On another occasion He said to me : " I have chosen thee to be My spouse, and we pledged each other fidelity when thou didst make thy vow of Chastity. It was I Who urged thee to make it, before the world had any share in thy heart, because I wished to have it quite pure and unsullied by any worldly affections ; and in order to preserve it thus, I removed all malice from thy will so that it should not be corrupted.

" I then confided thee to the care of My Holy Mother, that she might fashion thee according to My designs."

22. He confides her to the care of the Blessed Virgin. And truly, she has always shown herself a good Mother to me, nor has she ever refused me her help. In all my troubles and needs I had recourse to her with the greatest confidence, for it seemed to me that I had nothing to fear under her maternal protection. Therefore, I made a vow at that time to fast every Saturday and to recite her Office of the Immaculate Conception as soon as I was able to read it ; I also promised to say daily, during my whole life, seven Ave Marias, making seven genuflections in honour of her seven Dolours, and I gave myself to her as her slave, begging her not to refuse to accept me in this capacity. I spoke to this good Mother quite simply as a child and henceforth felt for her a truly tender affection.

She reproved me, however, severely when she saw me about to give way to the terrible struggle that I felt within me. For, being no longer able to resist the solicitations of my family and the tears of my mother, whom I loved so tenderly, and who kept telling me that a girl ought to marry at the age of twenty, I began to fall in with her views. Satan, too, said to me con-

tinually: "Poor wretch, what do you mean by wishing
to be a nun? You will become the laughing stock
of the world, for you will never be able
to persevere, and how ashamed you
will be, when you put off the religious
habit and leave the Convent! Where
will you then go to hide yourself?"
Amidst all this I shed bitter tears, for
owing to the great distaste I had for marriage, I knew
not what to do, till at last my Divine Master, who always
kept my vow before my eyes, had pity on me.

**23. She lets her-
self be almost over-
come by affection
for her relations,
and by the deceit
of the evil one.**

One day after Communion He showed me, if I am not
mistaken, that He was the most beautiful, the wealthiest,
the most powerful, the most perfect
and the most accomplished amongst
all lovers. After having pledged my-
self to Him for so many years, how came it, said He,
that I now sought to break with Him for another? "Oh!
be assured that, if thou dost Me this wrong, I will
abandon thee for ever; but, if thou remainest faithful
to Me, I will never leave thee, I Myself will be thy
victory over all thy enemies. I pardon thy ignorance
because, as yet, thou dost not know Me; but, if thou art
faithful to Me and followest Me, I will teach thee to know
Me, and I will manifest Myself to thee." While He was
thus speaking, He spread such great calm over my interior
and filled my soul with such deep peace, that I resolved
henceforth to die rather than to change. It then seemed
to me that my bonds were broken, and that I had nothing
more to fear, for I thought that, if the religious life were
(a purgatory),[1] it would be easier for me to purify myself

**24. Our Lord re-
stores her peace.**

[1] These words which are omitted in the Autograph, doubtless
correspond with the idea of the servant of God.

therein during the remainder of my life, than to see myself cast into that hell which I had so often merited by my grievous sins and resistance.

Having thus decided for the religious life, the Divine Spouse of my soul, fearing lest I should again escape Him, asked me whether, considering my weakness, I would agree to His taking possession and making Himself Master of my liberty. I willingly consented, and from that time forth He took such firm hold of my liberty that I never more enjoyed the use of it. From that moment He penetrated so gently and deeply into my heart that I renewed my vow, which I now began to understand. I told Him that, if it were to cost me a thousand lives, I would never be anything but a religious; this I now openly declared, asking that all suitors should be dismissed, no matter in how advantageous a light they were represented to me. Seeing me so resolute, my mother shed no more tears in my presence, but she did so continually with all who spoke to her of it; and they did not fail afterwards to tell me that, as she had no one to attend her, I should be the cause of her death if I left her, and that I should have to answer for it before God, adding that I could be a religious just as well after her death as during her lifetime. One of my brothers,[1] who had a special affection for me, made every effort to turn me from my purpose, offering to assist me with his own means to a better settlement in the world. But my heart had become as insensible as a rock to all this, although I had to remain three years longer in the world.

I was now sent to one of my uncles[2] whose daughter[3]

25, She will be a religious in spite of all.

[1] Chrysostome Alacoque.
[2] This was Philibert Lamyn, brother of Madame Alacoque.
[3] Sister Saint-Colomb, Ursuline at Mâcon.

was a religious, and who, knowing that I, too, desired to be one, did all she could to induce me to join her ;

26. They try to induce me to enter the Ursulines at Mâcon. but not feeling drawn to the Ursulines, I said : "If I were to enter your Convent, it would only be through affection for you, whereas I wish to go to one, where I shall have neither friend nor acquaintance, so that I may be a religious only for the love of God." As, however, I was unacquainted with any other religious Order, I was at a loss to know where to go, and began to fear that I must yield to her importunities, the more so as I loved this cousin very much. She, on her side, made use of the authority which, as my guardian, my uncle had over me, and I dared not resist him. He loved me as one of his own children, and it was for this reason that he wanted to have me near him, and would not allow my brother to take me home, saying that he meant to conquer me. My brother, who had never consented to my desire to be a religious, was much displeased with me, for he imagined that I was agreeable to all this and that I wanted to enter the Ursulines in spite of him and without the consent of my family. But this was far from my thoughts, for, the more I was pressed to enter, so much the greater was my aversion to do so, and a secret voice said to me : "It is not there that I would have thee, but at 'the Holy Maries.' " [In French : Les Sainte-Maries].

I was not allowed, however, to visit them, although I had several relations there, and I **27. They wish to turn her from the Visitation.** was told things about them capable of discouraging the most resolute mind. But the more they tried to dissuade me from joining them, so much the more I liked them and felt my desire to enter there increase, owing to the sweet name of 'Holy Mary' which made me feel that I should find therein what I was seeking.

Once when I was looking at a picture of the great Saint Francis of Sales, it seemed to me that he called me 'his daughter' and cast upon me a look so full of paternal love that I no longer regarded him otherwise than as 'my good father.' But I did not dare mention this, and knew not how to withdraw myself from my cousin and her Community, who gave me such proofs of affection that I could no longer withstand them.

As they were ready to open the convent door to me, I received the news that my brother was very ill and my mother at death's door. I was conse-
28. She is suddenly recalled home. quently obliged to leave at once and go home without their being able to prevent me, although at the time I was ill myself, more in consequence of being forced to enter a Convent to which I did not feel called by God, than from anything else. I travelled all night, the distance being about ten leagues. In this manner I was released, but only in order to take up again a heavy cross, which I will not specify, having already written enough on the subject. Suffice it to say that all my former sufferings were redoubled. I was again told that my mother could not live without me, since my having been away for so short a time had been the cause of her illness, and that I should have to answer before God for her death. This being said to me by ecclesiastics, and my affection for my mother being so great, I was deeply grieved, and the devil took advantage of this to make me believe that it would be the cause of my eternal damnation.

On the other hand, my Divine Master urged me so powerfully to leave all and to follow Him, that I had no longer any rest. He also inspired me with so ardent a desire to conform myself to His suffering life, that all I endured seemed to be as nothing. This made me redouble my penances, and, prostrating myself at times at the foot of my crucifix, I said : " How happy should I be, O my dear Saviour, if Thou wouldst imprint on me the likeness of Thy sufferings ! " To which He replied : " This is what I intend to do, provided that thou dost not resist Me and that thou on thy side dost contribute thereto."

29. Conformity with Christ Suffering.

In order to give Him some drops of my blood, I then bound my fingers tightly and pierced them with needles ; and, during Lent, I took the discipline every day for as long a time as I was able, in honour of the strokes He received during His scourging, but however long a time I took it, I was scarcely able to offer any blood to my good Master in return for that which He had shed for love of me. As it was on the shoulders that I scourged myself, I required much time for it. But during the three days of Carnival, I would have wished to tear myself to pieces in reparation for the outrages perpetrated against His Divine Majesty by sinners; I fasted on those days, as much as possible, on bread and water, and the food which was given to me, I gave to the poor.

My greatest joy in the prospect of leaving the world was the thought that I should be able to receive Holy Communion frequently, which up to then I had not been permitted to do. I would have thought myself the happiest

30. Her ardent desire for Holy Communion.

person on earth, had I been allowed to do so often and pass the nights alone before the Blessed Sacrament. For, when there, I felt so safe that, though I was of an extremely timid nature, I forgot all my fears as soon as I was in this place of my delight. On the eves of Communion I found myself rapt in so profound a silence, on account of the greatness of the action I was about to perform, that I could not speak without great effort; and afterwards I would have wished neither to eat nor drink, to see nor speak, owing to the greatness of the consolation and peace which I then felt. I therefore used to hide myself in order to learn how to love my Sovereign Good, Who so strongly urged me to return Him love for love. But I thought that I could never love Him enough no matter what I did, unless I learnt how to meditate. I knew only what He had taught me concerning prayer, namely: to abandon myself to all His holy inspirations, whenever I was able to shut myself up in some little corner alone with Him. But I was not allowed enough leisure for this, because I was obliged to work all day with the servants, and when evening came, it seemed that I had done nothing to satisfy those with whom I lived. They inveighed so loudly against me that I had not the courage to eat, and I withdrew in order to have a few moments of that peace for which I so much longed.

But, as I complained unceasingly to my Divine Master that I dreaded not pleasing Him in all that I did (there being too much self-will and self-pleasing in my mortifications, whereas I valued only that which was done in obedience), I used to say to Him: "Alas! my Lord, give me someone who will lead me to Thee!" "Am I not sufficient for Thee?" He replied; "what dost thou

fear ? Can a child loved as much as I love thee perish
in the arms of a Father Who is Omnipotent ? "

I did not know what ' direction ' meant ; but I felt
an ardent desire to obey, and in His Goodness, my Divine

**31.   Jubilee Con-
fession to a Fran-
ciscan Father.**

Master permitted that, on the occasion
of a Jubilee, a Franciscan Father should
come to our house, and remain for the
night that we might have an opportun-
ity of making our general Confessions. I had written
mine about a fortnight before, for although I was in the
habit of making a general Confession whenever I had
an opportunity, it seemed to me that I could never do
so often enough on account of my great sins. I felt
such lively sorrow for them that not only did I shed many
tears, but in the excess of my grief, I would willingly
and with all my heart have published them to the whole
world. My greatest anguish arose from the fact that I
was so blinded as not to be able to recognize them, nor
express myself in such a manner as to show their full
enormity. Consequently, I wrote down all that I could
find in books which treated of Confession, sometimes
including sins, the mere utterance of which filled me
with horror. But I said to myself : " It may be that I
committed these sins without knowing or I may have
forgotten them, and it is but right that I should have the
confusion of accusing myself thereof, in order to make
satisfaction to the Divine Justice." It is true that, had
I believed myself guilty of the things of which I accused
myself, I should have been inconsolable ; and the mere
thought of those Confessions would ever after have been
a cause of grief to me, if My Divine Master had not
assured me that He pardoned all to a will free from
malice. When I made my Confession to that good

Father, he made me pass over several sheets of paper without allowing me to read them, although I begged him to permit me to satisfy my conscience, being a greater sinner than he thought me to be.

I was in great peace after this Confession. I also told the Father somewhat of my manner of life, concerning which he gave me much good advice. I did not venture, however, to say all, fearing it would be through vanity of which I was much afraid, being naturally inclined thereto. It seemed to me that all I did was through a motive of vanity, for I was not able to distinguish between feeling and consenting. I suffered much in consequence, for I had a dread of sin separating my soul from God. The good Father promised me some instruments of penance. I told him that my brother had kept me in the world for the space of four or five years during which time I had constantly thought of becoming a religious. Thereupon he remonstrated so much with my brother that the latter afterwards asked me whether I still had the intention of entering religion, and when I replied that I would rather die than change, he promised to satisfy me in the matter.

He went, therefore, to make arrangements about my dowry with my cousin, who still continued to harass me, and my mother and relations also **32. Steps are taken to place her with the Ursulines.** wished me to enter that Convent. I was at a loss to know how to prevent it, but while my brother was away, I had recourse to the Blessed Virgin, my good Mistress, through the intercession of Saint Hyacinth to whom I prayed, and I had several Masses said in honour of my holy Mother, who, to console me, said lovingly : " Fear nothing, thou shalt be my true daughter, and I will always be thy good Mother." These words calmed me so much that I had not the least doubt of their realization in spite of all opposition. On his return, my brother said : " They ask four thousand [livres],[1] it remains for you to do as you please with your money, for nothing as yet has been settled." I replied in a decided manner : " It will never be settled, for I wish to go to ' the Holy Maries,' in a distant Convent where I shall have neither relations nor friends, because I desire to be a religious for the love of God alone. In leaving the world, I will do so wholly and entirely and will hide myself in some little nook in order to forget it, to be forgotten by it and to see it no more."

Several Convents were proposed, but I could not make up my mind about them ; as soon, however, as they mentioned Paray, my heart was **33. She chooses** overjoyed and I consented at once. But **the Visitation. She** I had yet a severe trial to undergo, for **is drawn to Paray** I was obliged to go and see the nuns **at the outset.** with whom I had been when eight years old. They took me into the Convent, called me their child and asked why I wanted to leave them, adding that they loved me dearly, and could not bear to see me enter the ' Holy Maries,' for they were convinced I should not persevere. I told them I would try and they made me promise to return to them when I left, for they said they were sure I would never be able to settle down. But in spite of all that was said, my heart remained insensible, and was more than ever confirmed in its resolution, ever repeating : " Either die or conquer."

[1] An old French coin the value of which differed in various parts of the country. Later on, it was replaced by the franc.

But I will pass over all the other conflicts I had to sustain, in order to arrive more quickly at the place of my happiness, ' my dear Paray,' where, as soon as I entered the parlour, I heard interiorly these words : " It is here that I would have thee to be."[1] Turning to my brother, I told him he would have to settle everything at once, for I should never go elsewhere. This surprised him all the more because he had taken me there merely to see the nuns of ' Holy Mary ' without letting it be known that I wanted to be one of them, and I had promised him this. However, I would not return home until everything had been settled. Thereupon it seemed to me that I began a new life, so great was the peace and happiness that I felt. I appeared so gay that those who knew nothing of what was going on, said : " Look at her, she is not much like a religious! " and in truth, I wore more trinkets than I had ever done before, and took part more frequently in amusements, on account of the great joy which I felt at seeing myself wholly and entirely belonging to my Sovereign Good. While I am writing this, my good Master often makes me this loving reproach : " See, My daughter, whether thou canst find a father, whose love for his only son has prompted him to take such care of him or show him such delicate proofs of his love, as are those which I have given and will yet give to thee of Mine ; for from thy tenderest years it has borne kindly with thee, and has trained and formed thee after My own manner, awaiting thee patiently, without being disheartened in the midst of all thy resistance. Remember, therefore, if

(marginal note:) 34. Her dear Paray. " It is here I would have thee to be."

[1] This first visit of Margaret to the parlour of the Visitation at Paray was on May 25th, 1671.

ever thou shouldst be unmindful of the gratitude thou owest Me and not refer the glory of all to Me, it would be the means of màking this inexhaustible source of all good dry up for thee."

At last the long-wished-for day dawned on which I was to bid farewell to the world. Never before had I felt such joy and firmness of purpose, for my heart seemed to be insensible to all the marks of affection and sorrow which were lavished upon me, especially by my mother, and I shed not a tear on leaving her. It appeared to me that I was like a slave who sees herself released from her prison and her chains, in order that she may enter the house of her Spouse to enjoy, without reserve, His presence, His wealth and His love. This is what He said to my heart which was overcome with joy, and I could give no other reason for my vocation to ' Holy Mary,' than that I wished to become a daughter of the Blessed Virgin. Nevertheless, I must own that when the moment of my entrance arrived, which was on a Saturday, all my former sufferings returned, which combined with various others made such a violent assault upon me that it seemed, on my crossing the threshold of the Convent, as though my soul were about to be separated from my body. Immediately after, however, I understood that Our Lord had cut off the sackcloth of my captivity and was clothing me with His robe of gladness.[1] In a transport of joy, I exclaimed : " It is here that God wills me to be ! " and I felt engraven on my mind the persuasion that this house of God was a

35. Margaret bids farewell to the world and enters the Monastery. June 12th, 1671.

[1] " Conscidisti saccum meum et circumdedisti me laetitia." Ps. xxix. 12.

holy place, that all who dwelt therein must be holy, and that the name of ' Holy Mary ' signified that I must become a Saint at any cost, abandoning and sacrificing myself to all without reserve or restriction. What sweetened the things that appeared most difficult to me in those beginnings was that every morning for some days, I was awakened by the following words, which I distinctly heard, although I did not understand them: *Dilexisti justitiam*, and the remainder of the verse ; and at other times : *Audia filia et vide*, etc. ; and again : " Thou hast known thy path and thy way, O my Jerusalem, house of Israel ! but the Lord will guide thee in all thy ways and will never abandon thee." All this I told my good Mistress,[1] without understanding it, for I looked upon her and my Superior[2] as upon my Lord Jesus Christ on earth. As I had never known what it was to be guided and directed, I was happy to find myself in a state of dependence, so that I might be able to obey, and I considered all that was said to me as so many oracles, feeling that I should have nothing to fear when acting under obedience.

As I asked my Mistress to teach me how to make mental prayer for which my soul hungered so greatly, she could scarcely believe that, having **36. The blank canvas.** entered religion at the age of twenty-three, I knew not how to make it. Upon my assuring her of my ignorance, she said: " Go and place yourself before Our Lord like a blank canvas before a painter." Not understanding what she meant, I would have liked her to explain, but I dared not ask

[1] Sister Anne-Françoise Thouvant, novice-mistress.
[2] Mother Marguerite-Hiéronyme Hersant, professed Sister of the first Monastery of Paris. She governed that of Paray from 1666 to 1672.

her to do so; however, an interior voice said to me: "Come, and I will teach thee." As soon as I went to prayer, my Sovereign Master gave me to understand that the canvas was my *soul* whereon He wished to paint all the features of His suffering life, which had been spent wholly in love, silence, privation and solitude, and finally had been consummated in sacrifice. These characters He would imprint on my soul, after having purified it from all the stains with which it was as yet sullied, both through the love of self, and through affection for earthly things and for creatures to whom my compliant nature was much drawn.

At that moment He deprived me of everything, and after having emptied my heart and laid bare my soul, He enkindled therein such an ardent desire to love Him and to suffer that I no longer had any rest. He pursued me so closely that I had no leisure except to think of how I could love Him by crucifying myself. His goodness towards me had ever been so great that He has never failed to provide me with means of doing so.

Although I concealed nothing from my Mistress, I nevertheless formed the design of extending her permissions with regard to penances, and of going beyond her intention. When in the act of doing this, our Holy Founder interposed and gave me so severe a reproof that I have never since had the courage to recommence. His words remained deeply engraven on my heart: "What is this, my daughter, dost thou think to please God in surpassing the limits of obedience, which is the foundation and principal support of this Congregation, and *not* austerities?"

37. Her too great eagerness for penance. She is brought back to obedience by Saint Francis of Sales.

Thus I spent the time of my probation, animated with an ardent desire to belong entirely to God, Who in

38. Her Clothing. (August 25th, 1671.)

His mercy was ever urging me on in order to make me attain this happiness. When at length I received our Holy Habit, my Divine Master gave me to understand that now was the time of our espousals by which He acquired a new right over me, and that I was now doubly bound to love Him with a love of preference. He gave me further to understand that, after the manner of the most passionate of lovers, He would, during that time, allow me to taste all that was sweetest and most delightful in the tokens of His love, which were indeed so excessive, that I was often quite overcome thereby and incapable of acting. This was a cause of such confusion to me that I did not dare show myself, for which I was reproved and told that such was not the spirit of the daughters of Holy Mary which admitted of nothing extraordinary and that, unless I renounced it all, I could not be received.

This distressed me greatly, and I made every effort and spared no pains to withdraw from this way, but

39.   Efforts are made to keep her in the ordinary ways of the spiritual life.

all my efforts were in vain. My good Mistress contributed also on her part, but without my understanding it. Do what I would, I found it impossible to follow the method of prayer presented to me and was always constrained to return to that of my Divine Master, although I made every effort to forget all and turn away from Him. Seeing this and knowing how I hungered after mental prayer and longed to learn how to make it, I was given as aid to a Sister who made me work during the time of meditation, and when I asked my Mistress to be allowed to make it at another hour, she reproved me severely, saying that I could make my prayer while working during the exercises of the novitiate. I did so, and the sweet joy and consolation which my soul experienced was in no way diminished but on the contrary was ever more increased. I was ordered to hear the points of meditation in the morning, after which I was to leave the choir and employ the time in sweeping until Prime. I was then required to give an account of my prayer, or rather of that which my Sovereign Master made in me and for me. In all this I had no other object in view but to obey; in doing so I felt an extreme pleasure despite any bodily suffering which might result therefrom. At such times, I was wont to sing:

> The more my love they contradict,
>   The more love's flame towards Him doth tend;
> Though day and night they me afflict,
>   My soul from Him they ne'er can rend.
> Though suff'ring e'er should be my part,
>   He'll draw me closer to His Heart.

Although my sensitive nature felt keenly all humiliations and mortifications, I nevertheless had an insatiable desire for them, and I was constantly urged by my Divine Master to ask for them. This procured me a few good ones, for although I was refused those for which I had asked, as being unworthy to perform them, others that I little expected were imposed upon me, and these were so opposed to my natural inclinations that, in the violence of the efforts I had to make, I was constrained to say to my Good Master: "Alas! my God, come to my help, since Thou art the cause of them!"

40. Her thirst for humiliations and mortifications.

This He did, saying : "Acknowledge that thou canst do nothing without Me, Who will never let thee lack help, as long as thou keepest thy weakness and thy nothingness lost in My strength."

I will mention only one of these occasions of mortification which seemed to be beyond my strength, and in **41. Heroic efforts to overcome a natural repugnance.** which He truly permitted me to feel the effect of His promise. It concerned something for which our whole family had so great a natural aversion that, when making arrangements for my reception, my brother requested that it should never be asked of me. As the matter was indifferent in itself, consent was easily given. It was on this point that I was asked to overcome myself ; everyone harassed me so much about it, that I knew not on what to decide, the more so as it seemed to me that it would be a thousand times easier to sacrifice my life ; and if I had not cherished my vocation more than my life, I would have been prepared to renounce it rather than resolve to do what they desired of me. But it was useless to resist, since my Sovereign Master asked of me this sacrifice, on which so many others depended. For three days I struggled so violently that I excited the compassion of all, especially of my Mistress ; I did my utmost to do as she told me, but then my courage failed, and I nearly died of grief at not being able to overcome my natural aversion. "Alas ! " I said, " take away my life rather than let me fail in obedience ! " Whereupon she sent me away with these words : " I see you are not worthy to practise obedience ; I now forbid you to do what I had ordered you." That was enough for me. " Either die or conquer ! " I said, and going before the Blessed Sacrament, my usual place of refuge, I remained

about three or four hours imploring with tears and groans
the strength to overcome myself. "Alas! O my God,
hast Thou abandoned me? Must there still be some
reserve in my sacrifice instead of its being wholly consumed as a perfect holocaust!" But my Lord, wishing
to try to the utmost the fidelity of my love for Him, as
He afterwards showed me, took pleasure in watching the
conflict going on in His unworthy slave between Divine
Love and natural repugnance. At last, however, He
was victorious, for without any other consolation or
arms than these words: "There must be no reserve in
love," I went to my Mistress, and kneeling before her, I
begged her to allow me in pity to do what she had
desired of me. I did it at last, although I never in my life
felt so great a repugnance to anything, and the same was
renewed each time I had to repeat the act during the
following eight years or thereabouts.

After this sacrifice, my Sovereign Lord redoubled His
graces and favours which inundated my soul to such an
extent that I was frequently forced to
cry out: "O my God, stay this torrent
which overwhelms me or increase my
capacity to receive it!" But I will omit
mentioning here all His predilection for
me and those outpourings of pure love, which were so
great that I should not be able to express them.

42. This sacrifice obtains for her a fresh abundance of graces.

All this gave rise to fresh trials as the time for my
Profession drew near. I was told that it was evident I
was not capable of acquiring the spirit
of the Visitation, which feared all such
ways as are open to deception and illu-
sion. I represented this to my Sovereign,
to Whom I made the following com-

43. They have fears concerning her vocation. Our Lord becomes her surety.

plaint : "Alas ! my Lord, wilt Thou then be the cause of my being sent away ? " To which He replied : " Tell thy Superioress[1] that she need not fear to receive thee, that I answer for thee and that, if she will trust Me, I will be thy surety." On my telling her this, she ordered me to ask, as a proof of security, that He would render me useful to holy religion by the exact observance of all that is prescribed. To this His loving Goodness replied : " ' Tis well, my daughter, I grant thee all this, for I shall render thee more useful than she thinks, but in a manner known at present only to Me. Henceforth, I shall adjust My graces to the spirit of thy Rule, to the will of thy Superiors and to thy weakness ; so that thou must regard as suspicious everything that might withdraw thee from the exact observance of thy Rule, which it is My will that thou shouldst prefer before all else. Further, I am satisfied that thou shouldst prefer the will of thy Superiors to Mine, whenever they may forbid thee to do what I command thee. Suffer them to act as they please with thee ; I shall know well how to find means for the accomplishment of My designs, even though they may appear to be opposed and contrary thereto. I reserve for Myself only the guidance of thy interior, and especially of thy heart, for, having established therein the empire of My pure love, I will never yield it to others.' " Our Mother and my Mistress were satisfied with this promise, the effects of which were so manifest that they could no longer doubt that they were the words of the (Eternal) Truth ; for I had no interior disquietude, and my only desire was to obey, in spite of anything I might

[1] Mother Marie-Françoise de Saumaise, professed Sister of the Monastery of Dijon, elected Superioress of that of Paray at the Ascension of 1672.

have to suffer in so doing. Esteem and praise were for me an intolerable martyrdom, and I looked upon them as just chastisements for my sins which appeared to me so great that, in expiation for them and as a means of satisfying Divine Justice, all imaginable torments would have been to me sweet to bear.

Having at last attained the long desired happiness of holy profession, it was on that day that my Divine Master willed to receive me for His **44. Margaret Mary is professed. (Nov. 6th, 1672.)** Spouse, but in a manner that I find myself incapable of expressing. I will merely say that He adorned me and treated me like a spouse of Thabor. This to me was harder than death, seeing in myself no resemblance to my Spouse, Whom I beheld all torn and disfigured on Calvary. But He said to me : " Let Me do everything in its time ; for I will have thee now to be the sport of My love, treating thee according to its good pleasure, as children treat their playthings ; thou must, therefore, abandon thyself blindly and without resistance, allowing Me to please Myself at thy expense ; thou wilt lose nothing thereby." He promised never again to leave me, saying : " Be ever ready and disposed to receive Me, for henceforth, I will make My abode in thee that I may be able to hold familiar converse with thee."

From that time forward, He allowed me continually to enjoy His divine presence, in a manner which I had **45. She is gratified with a mysterious presence of her Divine Master.** not yet experienced. Judging by the effects which this has ever since produced in me, I had never received so great a favour. I saw and felt Him close to me, and heard His voice much better than if it had been with my bodily senses.

For in that case I could have diverted my attention and turned away from Him, but I could put no hindrance in the way of this impression which I had no share in producing in myself. It imprinted in me so deep a sense of self-annihilation, that I felt, as it were, sunk and annihilated in the abyss of my nothingness, whence I have not since been able to withdraw myself. Penetrated with respect for this infinite Majesty, I would have wished constantly to remain either prostrate on my face before Him, or on my knees, and indeed I always did so as far as my occupation and my weakness permitted, for He allowed me no rest in any less respectful posture, so that I never dared remain seated, except when in the presence of others.

At the same time, He gave me so deep an insight into my great unworthiness that I dared not show myself but with a strange feeling of confusion. I wished no longer to be remembered except to be despised, humbled and insulted; for this is all that I deserve. This treatment was so pleasing to the well-Beloved of my soul, that despite my pride and susceptibility He let me find no pleasure in creatures except when I met with these occasions of contradiction, humiliation and abjection, which it was His will should be my most delicious food, nor did He ever permit it to fail me or allow me to say: " It is enough." On the contrary, He Himself supplied what was wanting on the part of creatures or on my own. But, O my God, it was in a manner far more painful when Thou didst contribute Thy part ; this would take too long for me to explain.

He deigned to converse with me sometimes as a friend, at other times as a spouse passionately in love, again as a father who dearly loves His only child, or under other titles. I refrain from speaking of the effects this produced in me and will only mention that He revealed to me two *sanctities* in Him, the one of *love* and the other of *justice*, both rigorous in their degree, which would continually be brought to bear upon me. The former would make me suffer a most painful kind of purgatory, in order to relieve the holy souls therein detained whom, according to His good pleasure, He would permit to address themselves to me. And as for His sanctity of justice, which is so terrible to sinners, it would make me feel the weight of His just rigour by causing me to suffer for sinners, and " especially," He said, " for souls consecrated to Me, regarding whom I will in future make thee see and feel what thou must suffer for love of Me."

46. The two sanctities of love and of justice.

But, O my God, Thou Who knowest my ignorance and inability to express all that has since taken place between Thy sovereign Majesty and Thy poor unworthy slave by the ever-operative effects of Thy love and Thy grace, grant me the means of being able to say somewhat of that which is most comprehensible and tangible and which may show to what an excess of liberality Thy love has led Thee towards so miserable and unworthy an object.

As I held nothing back from my Superior and my Mistress, although it often happened that I understood nothing of what I told them, they impressed upon me that extraordinary ways were not suitable for the daughters of Holy Mary. I was deeply grieved at this and made every effort to turn aside from this way, but in vain, for the

47. She endeavours to turn aside from extraordinary ways and complains to Our Lord.

Spirit which led me had already gained such power over

mine, that not only my mind but all my interior powers were wholly absorbed in Him and I was no longer mistress of them. I did my utmost to follow the method of prayer and other practices which were taught me, but I was not able to retain anything. It was in vain that I read my points of meditation, for all vanished from my mind, and I could neither learn nor retain anything except what my Divine Master taught me. This was a cause of no little suffering to me, because they [i.e., her superiors] did their best to destroy His action within me, and I was ordered to do likewise.—I made every effort to resist Him, and followed minutely all that obedience demanded of me in order to withdraw me from His power which, however, rendered all my attempts useless. I then poured out my heart to Him, saying : " Why, O my Sovereign Master, why not leave me in the ordinary way of the daughters of Holy Mary ? Hast Thou then brought me to Thy holy house to destroy me ? I beseech Thee, give these extraordinary graces to such chosen souls as will correspond with them better and glorify Thee more than I do, for I only resist Thee. All I wish for is Thy love and Thy Cross, that suffices for me to become a good religious, which is all I desire." " Let us," He replied, " continue the conflict, My daughter, I am quite content to do so ; we shall see who will be victorious, the Creator or His creature ; Strength or weakness, the All-powerful or powerlessness ; but whoever is conqueror will remain so for ever." This filled me with deep confusion, whereupon He said : " Be assured that I am not by any means offended by all these struggles and the opposition thou dost make Me through obedience for which I gave My life ; but I will teach thee that I am the absolute Master of My gifts as also of My creatures, and nothing will be able to prevent Me from carrying out My designs. Therefore, not only do I desire that thou shouldst do what thy Superiors command, but also that thou shouldst do nothing of all that I order thee without their consent. I love obedience, and without it no one can please Me." This was so agreeable to my Superior that she told me to abandon myself to His guidance ; which I did, and my soul, which had hitherto suffered a cruel agony, was now filled with peace and joy.

After Holy Communion He asked me to renew the sacrifice I had already made Him of my liberty and of my whole being, and I did so with all my heart. "Provided, O my Sovereign Master ! " I said, "that Thou wilt never allow anything extraordinary to appear in me, but what may cause me

48. Our Lord again requires her to abandon herself to Him.

humiliation and abjection before creatures and lower me in their esteem. For, alas ! O my God, I feel my weakness, I fear to betray Thee, and that Thy gifts should not be in safety with me ! " "Fear nothing, My daughter," He replied, " leave all to Me, for I will constitute Myself the Guardian of them and render thee powerless to resist Me." "What then, my God ! Wilt Thou always let me live without suffering ? "

Immediately a large cross was shown me, the extremity of which I could not see, but it was all covered with flowers.

"Behold the bed of My chaste spouses on which I shall make thee taste all the delights of My pure Love. Little by little these flowers will drop off, and nothing will remain but the thorns,

49. The flowers. and the thorns of the cross. Three imperious desires.

which are hidden because of thy weakness. Nevertheless, thou shalt feel the pricks of these thorns so keenly that thou wilt need all the strength of My love to bear the pain." These words delighted me, as I thought I should never find enough suffering, humiliations or contempt to quench the burning thirst I had for them, and that I could never experience greater suffering than that which I felt at not suffering enough ; for my love for Him gave me no respite day or night. But I was distressed to be enjoying so much sweetness. I wished for the cross alone ; and in order to this I desired to see my body always over-whelmed with austerities of work, of which I did my share as far as my strength permitted ; for I could not live a moment without suffering. The more I suffered, the more I satisfied that sanctity of love, which had kindled three desires in my heart that unceasingly tor-mented me. The first was to suffer, the second to love Him and to receive Holy Communion, and the third to die in order to be united to Him.

I no longer cared for time or place, since my Sovereign Lord accompanied me everywhere. I was quite indiffer-ent to the use which was made of me, being certain that, as He had given Himself to me without any merit on my part, but solely through His goodness, He could consequently not be taken from me, and this made me happy everywhere. I experienced this when, during the retreat before my profession, I was made to look after an ass and its foal in the garden. This occupation gave me no little trouble, for I was not allowed to tie them up, and was ordered to keep them within the limits of a small corner that had been shown me, for fear they should do harm to the garden, but they did nothing but run about. I

50. She looks after the ass and foal of the Monas-tery during her retreat before Pro-fession, and re-ceives the grace of a burning love of the cross.

had no rest until the evening Angelus when I went in to supper; during a part of Matins I returned again to the stable to feed them. Still I was so happy in this employment that I should not have minded had it lasted all my life. My Sovereign Lord kept me company so faithfully, that all this exterior exercise did not distract me. At this time I received graces so signal that I had never before experienced anything similar, in particular a deep understanding of the mystery of His Sacred Passion and Death. But this is a fathomless abyss to write about, and fearing to be too lengthy, I refrain from doing so. I will only say that it has given me such an intense love of the cross that I cannot live a moment without suffering, but suffering in silence, without consolation, alleviation or compassion, and in fine dying with the Sovereing of my soul, overwhelmed by the cross of every kind of opprobrium, of sorrow and of humiliation, forgotten and despised by all. This has lasted all my life, which, through His mercy, has been entirely spent in this manner which is that of pure love, and He has always taken care to provide me abundantly with these viands, so delicious to His taste, that He never says: " It is sufficient."

One day, on account of some fault which I had committed, my Divine Master gave me the following lesson. " Learn," He said, " that I am a Holy Master and One that teaches holiness, I am pure and cannot endure the slightest stain. Therefore thou must act with simplicity of heart and with an upright and pure intention in My presence. Know that I cannot endure the least want of straightforwardness, and I shall make thee understand that, if the excess of My love has led Me to constitute

51. Exigencies of the Sanctity of God.

Myself thy Master, in order to teach and fashion thee after My manner and according to My designs, nevertheless I cannot bear tepid and cowardly souls, and, if I am gentle in bearing with thy weakness, I shall not be less severe and exact in correcting and punishing thy infidelities." He has made me experience this all my life. For I can say that He did not allow the smallest fault to pass, in which there was ever so little wilfulness or negligence, without correcting and punishing me for it, although always with His infinite mercy and goodness. Nevertheless, I own that nothing was more painful and terrible to me than to see Him ever so slightly displeased with me. All other sufferings, corrections and mortifications were nothing to me in comparison. Hence it was that I went promptly to ask a penance for my faults, for He was satisfied with those imposed upon me by obedience. The faults He reproved most severely were a want of respect and attention in presence of the Blessed Sacrament, especially during the Office and Mental Prayer ; a want of uprightness and purity of intention, also vain curiosity.

Although His pure and penetrating (Eyes) discover even the smallest faults against charity and humility in order to correct them severely, nevertheless nothing can be compared to a want of obedience either against Superiors or the Rules ; and the smallest reply to Superiors, manifesting repugnance to obey, is unbearable to Him in the soul of a religious. "Thou deceivest thyself," He said to me, "in thinking to please Me by actions and mortifications chosen by self-will which, rather than yield, prefers to make Superiors bend their will to it. O ! be assured, that I reject all such things as fruits corrupted by self-will

52. He rejects the works performed through self-will.

which I abhor in the soul of a religious. I would rather that she should take all her little comforts through obedience, than overburden herself with austerities and fasts through her self-will." When I happen to make such mortifications and penances of my own choice without His order or that of my Superior, He does not even allow me to offer them to Him. He reproves me for them, imposing a penance upon me as He does for my other failings, for each of which there is a particular punishment in the purgatory wherein He purifies me, in order to make me less unworthy of His divine Presence, of His communications and operations, for everything in me is done by Him. Having on one occasion finished taking the discipline for the space of an Ave Maris Stella, as I had been ordered, He said to me : " This is My share," but as I still continued, He added : "And that is the devil's," which made me cease at once. Another time when I was taking it for the Holy Souls in Purgatory and wanted to exceed the permission given me, they immediately surrounded me complaining that I was striking them. This made me resolve to die rather than overstep, ever so little, the limits imposed by obedience. He afterwards made me do penance for my fault. But nothing seemed difficult to me, because, at that time, He kept all the rigour of my troubles and sufferings absorbed in the sweetness of His love, which sweetness I often besought Him to withdraw from me, that I might relish the bitterness of His anguish and dereliction, of His agony and opprobrium and of His other torments. But He told me that I was to submit indifferently to all His various intentions and not lay down the law for Him. "I will make thee understand hereafter," He said, " that I am a wise and learned Director, Who knows how to lead souls safely when they abandon themselves to Me and forget themselves."

One day, having a little more leisure,—for the occupations confided to me left me scarcely any—I was praying before the Blessed Sacrament, when I felt myself wholly penetrated with that Divine Presence, but to such a degree that I lost all thought of myself and of the place where I was, and abandoned myself to this Divine Spirit, yielding up my heart to the power of His love. He made me repose for a long time upon His Sacred Breast, where He disclosed to me the marvels of His love and the inexplicable secrets of His Sacred Heart, which so far He had concealed from me. Then it was that, for the first time, He opened to me His Divine Heart in a manner so real and sensible as to be beyond all doubt, by reason of the effects which this favour produced in me, fearful, as I always am, of deceiving myself in anything that I say of what passes in me. It seems to me that this is what took place: " My Divine Heart," He said, " is so inflamed with love for men, and for thee in particular that, being unable any longer to contain within Itself the flames of Its burning Charity, It must needs spread them abroad by thy means, and manifest Itself to them (mankind) in order to enrich them with the precious treasures which I discover to thee, and which contain graces of sanctification and salvation necessary to withdraw them from the abyss of perdition. I have chosen thee as an abyss of unworthiness and ignorance for the accomplishment of this great design, in order that every thing may be done by Me."

After this He asked me for my heart, which I begged

52. She rests upon the Breast of Our Lord Who for the first time reveals to her His Heart, inflaming hers with love.

Him to take. He did so and placed it in His own Adorable Heart where He showed it to me as a little atom which was being consumed in this great furnace, and withdrawing it thence as a burning flame in the form of a heart, He restored it to the place whence He had taken it saying to me : " See, My well-beloved, I give thee a precious token of My love, having enclosed within thy side a little spark of its glowing flames, that it may serve thee for a heart and consume thee to the last moment of thy life ; its ardour will never be exhausted, and thou wilt be able to find some slight relief only by bleeding. Even this remedy I shall so mark with My Cross, that it will bring thee more humiliation and suffering than alleviation. Therefore I will that thou ask for it with simplicity, both that thou mayest practise what is ordered thee[1] as also to give thee the consolation of shedding thy blood on the cross of humiliations. As a proof that the great favour I have done thee is not imagination, and that it is the foundation of all those which I intend further to confer upon thee, although I have closed the wound in thy side, the pain will always remain. If hitherto, thou hast taken only the name of My slave, I now give thee that of the beloved disciple of My Sacred Heart."

After such a signal favour which lasted for a long time, during which I knew not whether I was in heaven or on earth, I remained for several days, as it were, on fire and inebriated [with divine love] and so completely out of myself, that I had to do myself violence in order to utter a

54. As a sign she continues to suffer from a pain in her side, and she becomes " the disciple of the Sacred Heart."

[1] The Religious of the Visitation are recommended by their Constitutions to ask their Superior with confidence for all they think they require, whenever they " believe they have any necessity."

single word. The effort I had to make in order to join in recreation or to take food was so great that it was all I could do to overcome myself, which was a cause of considerable humiliation to me. I was not able to sleep, because of the pain of the wound, which is so precious to me; it produces such heat within me that it burns and consumes me alive. I also felt such a plenitude of God, that I could not explain myself to my Superioress, as I should have wished, regardless of any suffering and confusion which the recital of these favours might cause me. I would rather have accused myself of my sins before the whole world than speak of these graces on account of my extreme unworthiness. It would have been a great consolation to me had I been permitted to read aloud my general confession in the refectory, in order thereby to make known the depth of corruption which is in me, so that none of the favours I received might be attributed to me.

On the First Friday of each month, the above-mentioned grace connected with the pain in my side was renewed in the following manner: The **55. On the First Friday of each month the Sacred Heart is shown to her as a resplendent sun or a glowing furnace.** Sacred Heart was represented to me as a resplendent sun, the burning rays of which fell vertically upon my heart, which was inflamed with a fire so fervid that it seemed as if it would reduce me to ashes. It was at these times especially that my Divine Master taught me what He required of me and disclosed to me the secrets of His loving Heart. On one occasion, whilst the Blessed Sacrament was exposed, feeling wholly withdrawn within myself by an extraordinary recollection of all my senses and powers, Jesus Christ, my sweet Master, presented Himself to me, all resplendent with glory, His Five Wounds shining like so many suns. Flames issued from every part of His Sacred Humanity, especially from His Adorable Bosom, which resembled an open furnace and disclosed to me His most loving and most amiable Heart, which was the living source of these flames. It was then that He made known to me the ineffable marvels of His pure [love] and showed me to what an excess He had loved men, from whom He received only ingratitude and contempt. " I feel this more," He said, " than all that I suffered during My Passion. If only they would make Me some return for My love, I should think but little of all I have done for them and would wish, were it possible, to suffer still more. But the sole return they make for all My eagerness to do them good is to reject Me and treat Me with coldness. Do thou at least console me by supplying for their ingratitude, as far as thou art able." On my representing to Him my inability, He replied: " Behold, this will supply for all that is wanting to thee." And at the same time His Divine Heart being opened, there issued from It a flame so ardent that I thought I should be consumed, for I was wholly penetrated with it, and being no longer able to bear it, I besought Him to have pity on my weakness. " I will be thy strength," He said to me, " fear nothing, but be attentive to My voice and to what I shall require of thee that thou mayest be in the requisite dispositions for the accomplishment of My designs. In the first place thou shalt receive Me in Holy Communion as often as obedience will permit thee whatever mortification or humiliation

56. She is to supply for the ingratitude of men.

57. She must communicate as often as obedience will permit, especially on the First Fridays. She is to make the Holy Hour.

it may cause thee, which thou must take as pledges of My love. Thou shalt, moreover, communicate on the First Friday of each month.—Every night between Thursday and Friday I will make thee share in the mortal sadness which I was pleased to feel in the Garden of Olives, and this sadness, without thy being able to understand it, shall reduce thee to a kind of agony harder to endure than death itself. And in order to bear Me company in the humble prayer that I then offered to My Father, in the midst of My anguish, thou shalt rise between eleven o'clock and midnight, and remain prostrate with Me for an hour, not only to appease the divine anger by begging mercy for sinners, but also to mitigate in some way the bitterness which I felt at that time on finding Myself abandoned by My apostles, which obliged Me to reproach them for not being able to watch one hour with Me. During that hour thou shalt do what I shall teach thee. But listen, My daughter, believe not lightly and trust not every spirit, for Satan is enraged and will seek to deceive thee. Therefore do nothing without the approval of those who guide thee; being thus under the authority of obedience, his efforts against thee will be in vain, for he has no power over the obedient.

I lost all consciousness during that time and I no longer knew where I was. When they came to withdraw me, seeing that I could make no reply, nor even stand except with great difficulty, they led me to Our Mother.[1] On seeing me thus, as it were, completely beside myself, all burning and trembling on my knees before her, she mortified

58. Her Superior mortifies her and refuses her everything. Margaret Mary is seized with a violent fever.

[1] Mother de Saumaise.

and humbled me to the utmost of her power, which pleased me and filled me with incredible joy, for I felt so great a criminal and so full of confusion, that, however rigorously I might have been treated, it would have appeared to me all too mild. After I had told her, though with extreme confusion, what had taken place, she proceeded to humble me still more, and refused to allow me, for the time being, anything of what I believed Our Lord asked of me, regarding all that I told her only with contempt. This consoled me greatly and I withdrew in peace. However, the fire which consumed me threw me into a burning fever. But I felt too great pleasure in suffering to utter any complaint, nor did I say anything about it until compelled to do so by weakness. The doctor declared that I had been ailing a long time on account of this fever of which I had over sixty more attacks. Never did I experience so much consolation, because the extreme pain my body endured somewhat relieved the burning thirst I had for suffering. For that devouring fire could only be fed with the fuel of the cross, that is to say, with pain, contempt and humiliations of every kind ; yet I never experienced any suffering equal to that which I felt at not suffering enough. It was thought that I should die therefrom.

Our Lord still continued to favour me with His graces, and once, being overcome with exhaustion, I received what seemed to me, an incomparable favour. The Three Persons of the Adorable Trinity presented themselves to me and filled my soul with inexpressible consolation. But I cannot well explain what then occurred, except that it seemed to me the Eternal Father presented me with a very heavy cross

59. The Three Persons of the Blessed Trinity appear to her.

beset with thorns and surrounded with various instruments of the Passion and said to me: " See, My daughter, I make thee the same present which I made to My Beloved Son." "And I," said Our Lord Jesus Christ, " will fasten thee to the cross as I Myself was fastened to it and will bear thee faithful company." The Third Adorable Person then said, that, being Love Itself, He would purify and consume me thereon. My soul was filled with unutterable peace and joy, and the impression made upon it by the Divine Persons has never been effaced. They appeared to me under the form of three young men clad in white and radiant with light, all being of the same age, height and beauty. I did not understand then, as I have done since, the extent of the sufferings which all this signified.

Being ordered to ask Our Lord for health, I did so, although with fear, lest my prayer should be heard. But I was told that my restoration to health **60. She is ordered** would be regarded as a certain sign that **to ask for health** what was passing within me was the **as a proof of the** work of the Spirit of God, in which **divine origin of her** case I should be allowed to do as He had **revelations.** commanded me, both with regard to Holy Communion on the First Friday of the month, and to watching, according to His desire, for an hour during the night between Thursday and Friday. Having by obedience represented all this to Our Lord, I did not fail to recover my health immediately. For the most Blessed Virgin, my good Mother, appearing to me, bestowed upon me many caresses, and, after having conversed with me for a long time, she said : " Take courage, my dear daughter, in the health which I restore to thee at the will of my Divine Son, for thou hast yet a long and pain-

ful way to go, always upon the Cross, pierced with nails
and thorns and torn with scourges. But fear nothing, I
will not abandon thee and I promise thee my protection."
A promise which she has since fully made me realize in
the great need I have had thereof.

My Sovereign Lord continued to favour me with His
real and sensible Presence, which grace, as I said above,
He promised would not be withdrawn
from me. And truly He never deprived
me of it for any fault I committed. But
as His sanctity cannot endure the slightest stain nor the least voluntary imperfection or one
caused by negligence, He shows me the smallest fault.
And since I am so imperfect and miserable as to commit
many, although involuntarily, I own that it is an intolerable torment to me to appear before this sanctity when
I have allowed myself to commit some act of infidelity.
There is no kind of torture which I would not endure,
rather than bear the presence of the All-holy God when
my soul is stained with some fault ; nay, I would rather
a thousand times plunge myself into a burning furnace.

61. The sanctity of God cannot endure the least stain.

On one occasion I yielded to a slight movement of
vanity in speaking of myself, but, O my God ! how many
tears and groans this fault caused me !
for, as soon as we were alone, He called
me to account in the following manner,
saying with a look of severity : " What
hast thou to boast of, O dust and
ashes, since of thyself thou art but
nothingness and misery, of which thou shouldst never
lose sight, and hence shouldst ever remain buried in
this abyss of thy nothingness ! In order that the greatness of My gifts may not lead thee to forget what thou

62. Our Lord shows her in a picture the sum-mary of all her misery.

art, I will set before thee thy portrait." Upon which He discovered to me this repulsive picture, which contained a summary of my whole being. It filled me with so much surprise and horror of myself that, had He not sustained me, I should have fainted with grief, and not being able to bear the sight thereof, I could not understand how, in the excess of His goodness and mercy, He had borne with me so long and had not already cast me into hell. This being the torture with which He punished the slightest movements of vain-glory in me, I was sometimes constrained to say to Him: "Alas! O my God! let me die or withdraw this picture from me; I cannot see it and live." For it produced in me feelings of intense hatred and vengeance against myself, and, not being permitted by obedience to treat myself as rigorously as these feelings urged me to do, I cannot express what I suffered. Knowing, however, that this Sovereign of my soul was satisfied with all that obedience required of me, and that He took a singular pleasure in seeing me humbled, I was very faithful in accusing myself of my faults that I might receive a penance for them. No matter how severe it might be, it was, so to say, an agreeable refreshment compared with that which He, Who discovered defects in what appeared to be the purest and most perfect, imposed upon me Himself. This He once gave me to understand on the Feast of All Saints, when I distinctly heard the following words:

Naught is sullied in innocence,
Naught is lost in power;
Naught passes away in this blest abode,
There all is made perfect in love.

The explanation of these words served me a long time as matter for meditation. " Naught is sullied in innocence "—that is to say, I was not to allow any stain to remain in my soul or in my heart. " Naught is lost in power "—by this I understood that I was to give and abandon everything to Him, Who is Power itself, and that one loses nothing by giving Him all. The other two lines referred to Paradise where nothing passes away, for everything there is lasting and is consummated in love. A slight glimpse of that glory was then revealed to me, and, O God ! into what a transport of joy and desire did it now throw me ! Being in retreat at the time, I spent the whole day in that ineffable delight, and it seemed to me that I had but to go and enjoy it at once. But I was very much mistaken, as the following words gave me to understand :

> In vain thy longing heart desires
>   To find an entrance there,
> Who to this heavenly bliss aspires,
>   On earth the cross must bear.

After which I was shown all that I would have to suffer throughout my whole life ; at this sight my whole being shuddered, although I did not from this picture understand it as fully as I have since done from subsequent events.

When I was preparing to make my annual confession and was anxious to discover my sins, my Divine Master said to me : " Why dost thou torment **63. God requires** thyself ? Do what lies in thy power, I **humility and sin-** will supply what is wanting. In this **cerity in confes-** Sacrament I ask for nothing so much as **sion.** for a contrite and humble heart which, with a sincere will never to offend Me again, accuses itself frankly. I then pardon without delay, and hence follows perfect amendment."

But as this Sovereign Spirit which acted in me independently of myself had assumed so absolute an empire over my whole spiritual and even physical being, it was no longer in my power to excite in my heart any emotion of joy or sorrow except according to Its good pleasure, nor to occupy my mind with other thoughts than those I received from It. This continually filled me with a strange fear of being deceived, whatever reassurance to the contrary I might receive either from God Himself or from those who guided me, namely from my superiors. When directors were given me, it was only to examine the spirit by which I was led, and full liberty was left to them to approve or disapprove of it. But to my grief, instead of withdrawing me from the state of deception in which I believed myself to be, my confessors and others plunged me still deeper into it. They told me to give myself up unreservedly to the power and guidance of this Spirit and allow myself to be led by It, even were It to permit that I should become the sport of the devil, as I might think, I must nevertheless not desist from following Its movements.

64. She fears that the Spirit by which she is led is not the Spirit of God.

I therefore made my annual confession, after which I seemed to see and to feel myself stripped and, at the same time, clothed with a white robe, while I heard these words : " Behold the robe of innocence with which I clothe thy soul, that thou mayest henceforth live only the life of a Man-God ; that is to say, that thou mayest live as no longer living, but allow Me to live in thee, for I am thy life, and thou shalt no longer live but in Me and

65. The robe of innocence.

by Me. My will is that thou shouldst act as no longer acting, leaving Me to act and work in thee and for thee, and abandoning all to My care. Thou must henceforth have no will, letting Me will for thee in everything and everywhere as though thou hadst none."

This only Love of my soul appeared to me once holding in one hand the portrait of the happiest life imaginable for the soul of a religious : a life of peace spent in the enjoyment of interior and exterior consolation, together with perfect health and the applause and esteem of creatures and many other things agreeable to nature. In the other hand He held the picture of a life poor and abject, continually crucified by all kinds of humiliations, contempt and contradictions, in fine a life of suffering in mind and body. He held out these two pictures to me saying : " Choose, My daughter, the one which pleases thee best. I will give thee the same graces with the one as with the other." Prostrating myself at His Feet to adore Him, I said : " O my Lord, I wish for nothing but Thee and am content with the choice Thou wilt make for me." After He had strongly urged me to choose, I exclaimed : " Thou art sufficient for me, O my God ! Do for me whatever will glorify Thee the most, having no regard either to my interest or satisfaction. It is sufficient for me to know that Thou art satisfied." Then He told me that, with Magdalen, I had chosen the better part which should not be taken from me, since it would be my inheritance for ever ; and presenting me with the picture of the crucifixion : " Behold," said He, " what I have chosen for thee ; this it is which is most agreeable to Me, both in order to accomplish My designs and to render thee conformable to Me. The other is a

66. Double picture of a happy life and of a crucified life.

life of enjoyment, not of merit: it is for eternity." I forthwith accepted this picture of crucifixion and death and kissed the Hand which offered it to me; and although my nature shuddered at the sight, I embraced it with all the affection of which I was capable. As I pressed it to my heart, I felt it so strongly imprinted on me, that I seemed no longer to be aught but a compound of all I had seen portrayed therein.

My dispositions were so changed that I no longer knew myself. But I abandoned myself entirely to the judgment of my Superior, from whom I could **67. God enlightens** conceal nothing, nor could I omit to do **the Superior as to** anything she ordered me, provided it **the manner in** proceeded directly from herself. But **which she should** the Spirit by Which I was possessed **direct her.** made me feel extreme repugnance when she ordered me to do anything or sought to direct me according to the advice of others, for my Divine Master had promised me always to give her the necessary light whereby to guide me according to His designs.

As it was at Holy Communion and during the night, especially that between Thursday and Friday, that I received from His goodness the most signal graces and inexpressible favours, Our Lord warned me once that Satan had asked to try me, like gold in **68. Satan is per-** the furnace, in the crucible of contradic- **mitted to tempt** tions and humiliations, of temptations **her.** and derelictions, and that He had given him full liberty with the exception of impurity.[1] Having such hatred for that vice, He would not allow him to trouble me on that score, even as He had

[1] See page 103, the exceptional temptation she had one day to endure on this point.

never permitted Satan to attack Him in the slightest way in that matter. But as for all other temptations, He said, I must be on my guard, especially against those of pride, despair and gluttony, of which I had a greater horror than of death. But He assured me I need fear nothing, as He would be as an impregnable fortress within me, that He would fight for me and surround me with His power that I might not succumb, and that He Himself would be the reward of my victories ; but, He added, I must continually watch over my exterior, whilst He reserved for Himself the care of my interior. It was not long before I heard the threats of my persecutor. For having presented himself to me under the appearance of a frightful Moor, his eyes flashing like two live coals and gnashing his teeth at me, he said : " Accursed that thou art, I will capture thee, and, if once I have thee in my power, I will make thee feel what I can do ; I will injure thee on every occasion." Although he threatened me in many other ways, I, nevertheless, feared nothing, so great was the interior strength that I experienced. It seemed to me that I should not have feared all the fury of hell, as I had by me a small crucifix to which my Sovereign Deliverer had given the power to drive from me all this infernal fury. I wore it constantly on my heart, both night and day, and received great solace therefrom.

I was at that time placed as aid in the infirmary where God alone knows all I had to suffer, both from my quick **69. She becomes** and sensitive nature as also from crea-
the butt of the per- tures and the devil. The latter would
secutions of Satan frequently make me fall and break what
and is sustained by I was carrying. Then he would mock
her angel guardian me, laughing in my face and saying :
who reproves her
when necessary. " Oh, thou clumsy creature, thou wilt

never do any good!" This made me so sad and dejected that I scarcely knew what to do; for he often rendered me powerless to tell Our Mother about it, because obedience overthrew and deprived him of all his power over me. Once when I was carrying a pan full of red-hot coals, he made me fall from the top to the bottom of a staircase without any of them being upset and without my sustaining the least injury; those who were present thought I must have broken my legs. But I felt my faithful guardian at my side, for I was often favoured with his presence, and he frequently reproved and corrected me. When I once sought to busy myself regarding the marriage of one of my relations, he represented this to me as unworthy of a religious, and he rebuked me severely for it, adding that, if ever again I meddled with this kind of intrigue, he would hide himself from me. He could not tolerate the least want of respect or modesty in the presence of my Sovereign Master before Whom I saw him prostrate on the ground, and he wished me to be so too. I prostrated as often as possible, for I found no posture better suited to relieve my continual sufferings of body and mind, since it was the most conformable to my nothingness, of which I never lost sight. I always felt engulfed therein, whether in desolation or in consolation, though in the latter I never experienced any pleasure.

This Sanctity of Love urged me so strongly to suffer in order to make Him some return, that I could find **70. The salutary bread of suffering.** no sweeter repose than to feel my body overwhelmed with pain, my mind plunged in dereliction and my whole being a prey to humiliations, contempt and contradictions. And these by the grace of God were not wanting to me, for He did not leave me a moment without them, either from within or from without. When this salutary bread was diminished, I was constrained to seek other nourishment by mortification ; and my proud and sensitive nature furnished me with ample matter. He wished that I should not lose a single occasion, and when I happened to do so by reason of the great violence I had often to use in order to overcome my repugnance, He made me pay doubly for it. When He desired something from me, He urged me so strongly that it was impossible for me to resist. This was a cause of much suffering to me, for I was often inclined to resist, as He took me by all that was most opposed to my nature and inclinations and wished that I should unceasingly act contrary thereto.

I was so extremely dainty that the least want of cleanliness made me feel inclined to vomit. He reproved me for this with such severity, that, on one **71. She overcomes her natural delicacy by heroic actions.** occasion, being about to remove what a sick person had vomited, I was constrained to take it up with my tongue and to swallow it, saying : " Had I a thousand bodies, O my God, a thousand loves and a thousand lives, I would immolate them all to Thy service ! " I experienced such delight in this action that I would have wished to meet every day with similar occasions, that I might thus learn to conquer myself, having God alone as witness. And He, Whose goodness alone had given me the strength to overcome myself, did not fail to manifest to me the pleasure He had taken therein. For the following night, if I mistake not, He kept me for two or three hours with my lips pressed to the Wound of His Sacred Heart. It would be difficult for me to explain what I then felt, and what marvellous effects this grace produced in my soul and in my heart. But this will suffice to make known the infinite goodness and mercy of my God towards one so miserable.

Nevertheless He did not wish that my sensitiveness and my repugnance should decrease, and this not only to honour the agony which He vouchsafed to feel in the Garden of Olives, but also to furnish me with matter for victory and humiliation.   But, alas ! I am unfaithful, I often fail, and He sometimes seemed pleased that I should do so, both to humble my pride and to make me distrust myself, seeing that without Him I could only do evil and would fall continually without being able to rise again. At such times this Sovereign Good of my soul would come to my assistance, and like a good father would stretch out His loving arms towards me, saying : " Now thou knowest full well that [thou canst do nothing][1] without Me." . This filled me with gratitude for His loving kindness, and I shed an abundance of tears on seeing that His only revenge for my sins and continual infidelities was an excess of love by means of which He seemed to wrestle with my ingratitude. He would sometimes place it before my eyes side by side with the multitude of His graces, thus making it impossible for me to speak to Him except by my tears, while I suffered more than I can express. Thus did this Divine Love deal with His unworthy slave.

It happened once, when I was tending a patient who was suffering from dysentry, I was overcome by a feeling of nausea ; but He gave me so severe a reprimand, that I felt urged to repair this fault. . . . [" The Saint

[1] These four words are torn in the original and have been supplied from another MS.

then performed an act so repulsive to nature that not only would no one have advised it, but no one would even have permitted it." Words taken from *Life of St. Margaret Mary*, Visitation Library, Roselands, Walmer, page 81.] He then said to me : " Thou art indeed foolish to act thus ! " " My Divine Master," I replied, " it was in order to please Thee, and to win Thy Sacred Heart Which, I hope, Thou wilt not refuse me. But Thou, O my Lord, what hast Thou not done to win the hearts of men, and yet they refuse them to Thee and often drive Thee from them ! " " It is true, My daughter, that My love has made Me sacrifice everything for them, and they make Me no return. But I wish thee to supply for their ingratitude by the merits of My Divine Heart.

" I will give thee My Heart, but thou must first constitute thyself Its holocaust, so that, by Its intervention, thou mayest turn aside the chastise-**72. Our Lord asks** ments which the Divine Justice of My **her for a painful** Father is about to inflict upon a re-**sacrifice on behalf** ligious community which in His just **of her community.** wrath He wishes to correct and chastise." Thereupon He showed it to me, together with the particular faults which had irritated Him and all that I should have to suffer in order to appease His just anger. I shuddered from head to foot and had not the courage to make the sacrifice. I replied that, not being at my disposal, I could not do so without the consent of obedience. But the fear I had of being made to do it led me to neglect speaking of it. He pursued me, however, unceasingly and left me no peace. I shed abundant tears, and at length I found myself constrained to make it known to my Superioress who, seeing my distress, ordered me to sacrifice myself without reserve to all that He required of me. But, O my God, my anguish was now redoubled, for I had not the courage to say 'yes,' and my resistance continued. But on the eve of the Presentation this Divine Justice appeared to me armed in so terrible a manner, that I was quite beside myself, and not being able to do anything in my own defence, it was said to me, as to Saint Paul : "*It is hard for thee to kick against the goad* of My Justice ! But since thou hast made so much resistance in order to avoid the humiliations that thou wouldst have to suffer in this sacrifice, I will give them to thee twofold. I asked of thee merely a secret sacrifice, but now it shall be public, at a time and in a manner beyond all human calculation, and accompanied by such humiliating circumstances, that they will be a source of confusion to thee for the rest of thy life, as well in thine own sight as in that of others, that thou mayest understand what it is to resist God."

73. Having at first resisted, the sacrifice is required of her under more painful conditions.

Alas, I understood it but too well, for never before had I been in such a state. Here are a few details, but not all. After the evening meditation, I was incapable of leaving the choir with the rest but remained there until the last bell for supper, giving vent to my anguish in tears and groans. I then went to collation, for it was the eve of the Presentation ; and, having dragged myself by main force to the community room, I felt so strongly urged to make this sacrifice aloud, and in the manner in which God gave me to understand He wished it to be made, that I was constrained to go in search of my Superioress who was ill at the time. But I confess that I was in such a troubled state that I seemed like a person bound hand and foot, to whom no freedom was left, either interior or exterior, save tears ; these I shed in abundance, believing them to be the only outlet to my sufferings ; for I felt like a guilty criminal who was being dragged by cords to the place of torture. I beheld this Sanctity of God armed with the thunderbolts of His just anger, ready to hurl them at me, and to plunge me, as it seemed to me, into the gaping jaws of hell which I saw open and ready to swallow me up.

I felt consumed with a devouring fire, which penetrated even to the marrow of my bones, and my whole being was seized with a strange trembling, the only words I could utter being : " My God, have pity on me according to the greatness of Thy mercy ! " Overwhelmed with anguish I continued to sigh and groan, being utterly unable to go to my Superioress until about eight o'clock, when a Sister, having found me in this state, led me to her. She was extremely surprised at seeing me in a condition which, at the time, I was unable to explain, and, to add to my suffering, I believed that, on seeing me in this state, everyone would know the cause thereof, though such was not the case. My Superioress, knowing that obedience was all-powerful over the Spirit Which ruled me, ordered me to tell her my trouble. Thereupon I immediately told her of the sacrifice which God required me to make of my whole being in the presence of the community, and the reason for which He demanded it. This latter I will not express more definitely, for fear of wounding holy charity and at the same time the Heart of Jesus Christ, in Which this precious virtue has its source, and for which reason He wills that under no pretext whatever it should be impaired.

Having at length done what my Sovereign Lord desired of me, they spoke and judged of it in various ways ; but I leave all these circumstances to the Mercy of God. Truly it seems to me that if all I had suffered up to that time and all I have endured since, were united, and, thus combined, were to continue until my death, this suffering would not bear any comparison with that which I underwent that night, when I was dragged from place to place and subjected to the most fearful humiliations. Thereby Our Lord was pleased to gratify His miserable slave, that thus I might honour the agonizing night of His Passion, although what I endured was but a small sample of it.

74. The night of agony.

The night passed thus in torments known only to God, and without any rest, until about the time for Holy Mass next morning when I seemed to hear the following words : "At last peace is restored, and My Sanctity of justice is satisfied by the sacrifice thou hast made in honour of that which I made at the moment of My Incarnation in the womb of My Mother. I wished to renew and unite the merit thereof with this act of thine in order to apply it in favour of charity, as I have shown thee. Hence it is that thou must no longer lay any claim to whatever thou mayest do or suffer, either to increase thy merits or to make satisfaction by penance or otherwise, since everything is sacrificed in favour of charity. Therefore, in imitation of Me thou must act and suffer in silence without any other interest than the glory of God, in the establishment of the reign of My Sacred Heart in the hearts of men, to whom I wish to manifest It by thy means."

These sacred instructions were given me by my

Sovereign Lord after I had received Him, but He did not withdraw me from my state of suffering. I felt unalterable peace in the acceptance of all

75. She continues to suffer in order to appease the justice of God. I had to suffer, or would yet have to suffer, as was shown me, up to the day of judgment, if such were the Will of God. Indeed, He willed that I should appear no longer but as an object of contradiction, a very sink of vileness, of contempt and of humiliation which I beheld with pleasure overwhelming me on all sides, and that without any consolation, either human or divine. It seemed to me that everything conspired together to annihilate me. I was continually questioned, and the few answers they forcibly drew from me served as instruments to increase my torment. I could neither eat, speak nor sleep. My only repose and occupation consisted in remaining prostrate before my God, Whose sovereign Greatness kept me buried in the profound abyss of my nothingness, continually weeping, sighing and entreating Him that in His mercy He would turn away the scourge of His just anger.

The office in which I was employed at that time, by furnishing continual occupation both to mind and body, was a cause of unutterable torment to me, the more so as, despite all my sufferings, my Sovereign Master did not permit me to omit even the least of my duties. Nor would He allow me to ask dispensation therefrom or from anything prescribed by the Rule or observance, for the accomplishment of which I felt the strength of His sovereign Power dragging me like a criminal to the place of fresh torture. And this I found everywhere; for I was so lost and absorbed in my suffering that I no longer felt spirit or life but to see and feel what was painful to me. All this, however, caused me not the least movement of annoyance or disquietude, although amidst these troubles I was always led by what was the most opposed to unmortified nature and contrary to my inclinations.

It was observed that I ate nothing, for which I was severely reprimanded both by my Superioress and by my confessor, and they ordered me to eat **76. The refectory** everything that was set before me at **is a place of torture** table, an obedience which seemed **to her.** beyond my strength. But He Who did not let me want for help in the hour of need enabled me to submit and do so [without] reply or excuse, although after each meal I had to vomit the food I had taken. As this continued for some time, it caused me considerable suffering and pain, so that at last I could no longer retain anything of the little I took, even after it had seemed good to mitigate the order, by requiring me to eat only that which I felt I could digest. I must own that from that time the necessity to eat became a torment to me, and I went to the refectory as to a place of torture to which sin had condemned me. Nevertheless, in spite of the effort I made to eat indifferently whatever was presented to me, I could not refrain from taking what I thought to be the worst, as being more suitable to my poverty and nothingness, saying to myself that, as bread and water were sufficient for me, everything else was superfluous.

But to return to the state of suffering which instead of diminishing was constantly increased by the recurrence **77. They look** of painful humiliations : they thought **upon her as being** I was possessed or obessed by the **possessed by the** devil, and they threw a quantity of **devil.** Holy Water over me, and with the Sign of the Cross and other prayers they strove to drive away the evil spirit. But He by Whom I was possessed, far from taking flight, drew me yet more powerfully to Himself, saying : " I love Holy Water, and I have so great an affection for the Cross that I cannot refrain from uniting Myself closely with those who bear it like Me, and for the love of Me." These words enkindled in my soul so intense a desire of suffering that all that I endured seemed to me but a little drop of water which rather increased than allayed the insatiable thirst I felt. Nevertheless, it seems to me that I can truly say, there was no part of my being, either mind or body, which had not its own special suffering, and that without my receiving any pity or consolation ; the devil, too, assailed me with so much fury that I should have succumbed a thousand times had I not felt an extraordinary power within me sustaining me and combating for me amidst all that I have related. At last my Superior, not knowing what to make of me, ordered me to offer Holy Communion and in holy obedience ask Our Lord to restore me to my former condition. Having presented myself before Him as a holocaust, He said to me : " Yes, My daughter, I come to thee as a Sovereign Sacrificer to give thee renewed vigour in order to immolate thee to fresh sufferings." This He failed not to do, and I felt so great a change in me that I seemed like a slave who had just been emancipated. It did not, however, last long, for they began to tell me that the devil was the author of all that passed within me, and that, unless I were careful, he would, by his craft and cunning, bring about my eternal ruin.

This was a terrible blow to me, for I had always had a horror of deception and feared to deceive others unintentionally. Therefore I shed an abundance of tears, for I could not in any way withdraw myself from the power of that Sovereign Spirit Which acted within me ; and, despite all my efforts, I could not disengage myself from It, or prevent Its operations. For It had taken such possession of the faculties of my soul that I seemed to be in an abyss, and the greater the effort I made to emerge, the deeper I saw myself engulfed, although I made use of all the means which were suggested to me, but it was all in vain. The conflict was at times so great that I was quite exhausted. But my Sovereign Lord took pleasure in all this, and He reassured me so powerfully that my fears were instantly dispelled, when He said to me : " What hast thou to fear in the arms of the Almighty ? Could I possibly allow thee to perish and deliver thee up to thy enemies, after having constituted Myself thy Father, thy Master and thy Ruler from thy tenderest years and given thee continual proofs of the loving tenderness of My Divine Heart, in Which I have even established thy dwelling for time and for eternity ? As a greater assurance, say what stronger proof of My love thou wouldst have, and I will give it to thee. But why fightest thou against Me, Who am thy one, true and only Friend ? " These reproaches for my want of confidence filled me with such regret and confusion that I resolved henceforth not to contribute in any way towards the trials which would be made respecting the Spirit by Which I was led, but to accept humbly and willingly all that they wished to do with me.

O my Lord and my God, Who alone knowest the anguish I suffer in thus accomplishing this obedience, and the violence I must do myself to overcome the

78. She tries to free herself from the Spirit which governs her.

repugnance and confusion which I feel in writing all this, grant me the grace rather to die than to say anything but

79. Repeated expression of her repugnance to write her life.

what truly proceeds from Thy Spirit and which will give glory to Thee and bring confusion upon me. Mercifully grant, O my Sovereign Good, that these lines may never be seen by anyone but by him whom Thou wouldst have examine them, so that this manuscript may not prevent me from remaining buried in an eternal contempt and oblivion on the part of creatures. O my God, grant this consolation to Thy poor miserable slave! I forthwith received the following answer to my request: "Abandon everything to my good pleasure and let Me accomplish My designs, do not thou interfere in anything, for I will have care of all."

Therefore, O my God, I will continue through obedience, without any other object in view than that of satisfying Thee by the martyrdom which I suffer in writing this account, every word of which appears to me a sacrifice; but mayest Thou be thereby glorified eternally! It was in the following manner, however, that He manifested to me His will regarding this manuscript. I have always felt drawn to love my Soveriegn Lord for the love of Himself, neither wishing nor desiring anything but Him alone. I have never been attached to His gifts, however great they might be in my regard; I valued them only because they came from Him, and I reflected upon them as little as possible, trying to forget everything in order to remember Him alone, without Whom all the rest is nothing to me. When therefore, I was obliged to accomplish this obedience, I thought it would be impossible to write about what had happened so long ago; but my Lord has not failed to show me the contrary. In order to make it easier for me, He renews in me my former disposition concerning each point about which I am writing. This it is which convinces me that it is His will.

In the midst of all my fears and difficulties my heart, nevertheless, was always in a state of unalterable peace.

80. Our Lord sends her the Rev. Father de la Colombière. I was made to speak to certain theologians, who, far from reassuring me in my way, added still more to my difficulties, until at last Our Lord sent the Rev. Father de la Colombière here.[1] I had already spoken to him in the beginning of my religious life. My Sovereign Master had promised me shortly after I had consecrated myself to Him[2] that He would send me one of His servants, to whom He wished me to make known, according to the knowledge He would give me thereof, all the treasures and secrets of His Sacred Heart which He had confided to me. He added that He sent him to reassure me with regard to my interior way, and that He would impart to him signal graces from His Sacred Heart, showering them abundantly over our interviews.

When that holy man came and was addressing the community, I interiorly heard these words: " This is he whom I send thee." I soon realized this in the first confession on the Ember days[3]; for, although we had never either seen or spoken with each other, the Reverend Father kept me a very long time and spoke with me as though he understood what was passing within me. But I would not in any way open my heart to him just then, and, seeing that I wished to withdraw for fear of inconveniencing the community, he asked me if I would allow him to come and speak with me again in this same place.

[1] In 1679.   [2] In 1675.   [3] In Lent, 1675.

But in my natural timidity which shrank from all such communications, I replied that, not being at my own disposal, I would do whatever obedience ordered me. I then withdrew, having remained with him about an hour and a half. Before long he again returned, and although I knew it to be the Will of God that I should speak with him, I nevertheless felt an extreme repugnance to be obliged to do so. I told him so at once. He replied that he was very pleased to have given me an opportunity of making a sacrifice to God. Then, without trouble or method, I opened my heart and made known to him my inmost soul, both the good and bad ; whereupon he greatly consoled me, assuring me that there was nothing to fear in the guidance of that Spirit, since It did not withdraw me from obedience ; that I ought to follow Its movements, abandoning to It my whole being, sacrificing and immolating myself according to Its good pleasure. At the same time he expressed his admiration at the goodness of God, in not having been repelled by so much resistance on my part. He further taught me to value the gifts of God and to receive with respect and humility the frequent communications and familiar converse with which He favoured me, adding that I ought to be in a continual state of thanksgiving towards such infinite goodness. I told him that, as this Sovereign Lord of my soul pursued me so closely regardless of time or place, I was unable to pray vocally, and, although I did violence to myself in order to do so, I nevertheless remained sometimes without being able to pronounce a single word, especially when reciting the Rosary. He replied that I was not to force myself any more to say vocal prayers,

81. The Rev. Father reassures her and teaches her to value the gifts of God.

but to be satisfied with what was of obligation, adding thereto the Rosary when I was able. Having mentioned some of the more special favours and expressions of love which I received from this Beloved of my soul, and which I refrain from describing here, he said that in all this, I had great cause to humble myself and to admire the mercy of God in my regard.

But as this infinite Goodness did not wish that I should receive any consolation without its costing me many humiliations, this interview drew several upon me, and the Reverend Father himself had much to suffer on my account. For it was said that I wanted to deceive him and mislead him by my illusions, as I had done others. He was, however, in no way troubled by what was said, but continued none the less to help me, not only during the short time he remained in this town, but always. Many a time I have been surprised that he did not abandon me as others had done, for the way in which I acted towards him would have repulsed any other; he spared me, however, neither humiliations nor mortifications, which gratified me greatly.

One day when he came to say Mass in our church, Our Lord granted signal graces both to him and to me. As I went up to receive Him in Holy Communion, He showed me His Sacred Heart as a burning furnace, and two other hearts were on the point of uniting themselves to It, and of being absorbed therein. At the same time He said to me : " It is thus My pure love unites these three hearts for ever." He afterwards gave me to understand that this union was all for the glory of His Sacred Heart, the treasures of Which He wished me to reveal to him that he might spread them abroad, and

82. " Pure love unites these three hearts for ever."

make known to others their value and utility. To this
end He wished we should be as brother and sister, sharing
equally these spiritual treasures. Thereupon I represented to Him my poverty and the inequality which
existed between a man of such great virtue and merit, and
a poor wretched sinner like myself. But He replied: "The
infinite riches of My Heart will supply for and equalize
everything. Tell him this without fear." I did so in
our first interview. The profound humility and gratitude
with which he received this message and several other
things concerning himself, which I told him in the name
of My Sovereign Master, touched me so much, that I
profited more thereby than I would have done by all the
sermons I might have heard. I told him that Our Lord
granted me those graces only in order that He might be
glorified in the souls of those to whom I should distribute
them, either by word of mouth or by writing,—according
as He would make known to me His wishes—doing so
without any anxiety as to what I should say or write,
because He would attach the unction of His grace to
my words, in order to produce the effects He wished in
those who received them well. When I said that I suffered
much owing to the efforts I had to make in order to
write and give certain notes to persons from whom I
received great humiliations, he replied that, whatever
suffering and humiliation might ensue, I was never to
desist from following the sacred movements of that
Spirit. I was to say quite simply whatever It inspired me
or, if I had written it, to give the note to my Superior,
and then do whatever she would order me; this accord-
ingly I did, though it drew down upon me considerable
contempt on the part of creatures. He also ordered me
to write an account of what was taking place within me,

to which I felt extreme repugnance; for I wrote only to obey, and forthwith I burnt the manuscript, thinking I had sufficiently satisfied the command given me. But I suffered much on this account, for it was made a matter of conscience to me and I was forbidden to do so again.

83. Father de la Colombière orders her to write an account of what takes place within her.

On one occasion my Sovereign Sacrificer asked me to make in His favour and in writing a will or an entire and unreserved donation, as I had already done verbally, of all that I should do and suffer, and of all the prayers and spiritual goods which should be offered for me, either during my life or after my death. He bade me ask my Superior to act as notary in this deed, pledging Himself to pay her liberally, and saying that if she refused I was to address myself to His servant, the Rev. Father de la Colombière. But my Superior consented; and, when I presented the testament to this only Love of my soul, He expressed great pleasure, and said that He wished to dispose of it according to His designs and in favour of whomsoever He pleased. His love having despoiled me of everything, He did not wish me to have other riches than those of His Sacred Heart, of which He there and then made me a donation. He told me to write it in my blood according as He dictated it to me; I then signed it on my heart, writing thereon the Sacred Name of Jesus, with a penknife.

84. Deed drawn up by Mother Greyfié. In return Our Lord makes Margaret Mary a donation which she writes in her blood and signs on her heart in letters of blood. (Dec. 31st, 1678.)

He then said that, since I no longer had any claim to the good done to me, He would not fail to reward it a hundredfold, as though it were done to Himself. He told me further that He would bestow on her who had drawn up this deed in His favour the same reward as He had given to St. Clare of Montefalco ; and to this end He would add to her actions the infinite merits of His own enabling her thus, through the love of His Sacred Heart, to merit the same crown. This was a great consolation to me, for she was very dear to me, as she fed my soul abundantly with the delicious bread of mortification and humiliation, which was so agreeable to the taste of my Sovereign Master. In order to give Him this satisfaction I would have wished the whole world to contribute thereto. Hence God granted me the grace that mortification should never be wanting to me. My whole life has been passed in corporal sufferings, owing to my frequent illnesses and continual infirmities no less than to other causes. My soul also was continually suffering from dereliction and abandonment and from seeing God offended ; but in His goodness He has always sustained me amid persecutions, contradictions, and humiliations on the part of creatures, as well as amid temptations of the devil, who tormented and persecuted me greatly. He also fortified me against temptations proceeding from myself, who have been the most cruel of all my enemies and the most difficult to overcome.

For, in the midst of all that I have related, I was not spared work and occupation, as far as my strength permitted. It was no small suffering to me, in the state in which I then was, to believe that I was an object of aversion to others, and that they had great difficulty in bearing with me, since it was all I could do to bear with myself. All this caused me continual suffering in

85. Everything becomes a source of humiliation to her, without her being able to seek consolation elsewhere than in Our Lord.

my intercourse with my neighbour, and I had no other resource or remedy than the love of my own abjection. I had every reason to keep myself plunged therein, for everything, even the smallest action, brought upon me fresh humiliation. I was looked upon as a visionary, and as clinging obstinately to my illusions and imagination. In the midst of all these sufferings, I was not permitted to seek the least alleviation and consolation ; for my Divine Master did not allow it, desiring that I should suffer all in silence, and take the following as my motto :

> In silence shall my suffering be,
> Pure love from fear my soul doth free.

He willed that I should await all from Him ; and, if I happened to seek some little consolation, fresh torments and desolation were the only alleviation He permitted me to find. I have always looked upon this as one of the greatest graces my God has granted me. Another grace for which I would have wished to melt away with love, gratitude and thanksgiving towards my Deliverer is that He did not withdraw from me the precious treasure of the Cross, notwithstanding the bad use I have always made of it, which has rendered me most unworthy of so great a good. It was in these sentiments and amid the delights of the Cross that I exclaimed : " What shall I render to the Lord for the great blessings He has bestowed upon me ? " O my God, how great is Thy Goodness towards me in thus permitting me to sit at the table of the Saints, and partake of the same food with which Thou didst feed them. Thou dost give me to eat abundantly of the delicious viands of Thy intimate and most faithful friends, yes, even to me a wicked and miserable sinner ! "

Ah! I assure you that without the Blessed Sacrament and the cross I could not live, nor could I bear the length of my exile in this valley of tears, where I have never wished to see my sufferings diminish. The more overwhelmed my body was, the more my spirit rejoiced and was at liberty to be occupied with and united to my suffering Jesus, for I had no greater desire than to make of myself a true and perfect copy and representation of my Jesus Crucified. This is why I rejoiced when His sovereign Goodness made use of different artisans to aid according to His good pleasure in the perfecting of His work. But this Sovereign Lord did not depart from His unworthy victim, whose weakness and incapability for good He knew; and He would sometimes say to me: "I do thee a great honour, My dear daughter, in making use of such noble instruments to crucify thee. My Eternal Father delivered Me to be crucified into the hands of pitiless executioners, but in thy regard I make use of souls who are devoted and consecrated to Me, into whose power I have delivered thee and for the salvation of whom I wish thee to endure all that they will cause thee to suffer." This I did most willingly, always offering myself to suffer every chastisement due to any offence against God, which might be committed on my account. In truth, it did not seem to me that any injustice could be committed by causing me to suffer, since I could never have as much to bear as I deserved. But I own that I take such pleasure in speaking of the happiness of suffering, that it seems to me I could write whole volumes without being able to satisfy my desire, and my self-love finds much satisfaction therein.

86. " Without the Blessed Sacrament and the Cross I could not live." A perfect copy of Jesus Crucified.

On one occasion, my Sovereign Lord gave me to understand that He wished to withdraw me into solitude, not into the solitude of the desert, but into that of His Sacred Heart, where He wished to honour me with His most familiar converse like that of friend with friend; there He would give me further instructions regarding His Will and would renew my strength to enable me to fulfil it and to fight courageously until death, for I had still to sustain the attacks of several powerful enemies. That is why, in order to honour His fast in the desert, He willed that I should fast fifty days on bread and water. But not being allowed to do this, lest I should appear singular, He gave me to understand that it would be equally agreeable to Him, if I were to remain for fifty days without drinking, in order thereby to honour the burning thirst that His Sacred Heart had always endured for the salvation of sinners, as also that which He suffered on the tree of the Cross. I was allowed to perform this penance, which seemed to me more difficult than the former, owing to the great thirst with which I was continually tormented, making it necessary for me frequently to drink large cupfuls of water in order to quench it.

87. She passes fifty days without drinking in honour of Our Lord's thirst on the Cross.

During that time I endured great assaults on the part of the devil, who tempted me especially to despair. He represented to me that so wicked a creature as I should not presume to have a share in the joys of Paradise, since I already had none in the love of my God, of Whom I should be deprived for all eternity. This made me shed torrents of tears. At other times

88. She is violently tempted to despair, pride and gluttony.

Satan attacked me with thoughts of vain-glory, and finally with that abominable temptation of gluttony, making me feel excessive hunger, and then representing to me everything most apt to gratify the taste. As that happened during the time of my spiritual exercises, it became a real torment to me. This hunger lasted until I entered the refectory to take my repast, for which I immediately felt so great a disgust that I was obliged to do myself extreme violence in order to take a little food· As soon as I left the refectory, my hunger returned more violently than before. My Superior, from whom I concealed nothing of all that passed within me, on account of the great fear I always had of being deceived, ordered me to ask permission to eat whenever I suffered from great hunger. This I did, but with extreme repugnance, on account of the great shame I felt. Instead, however, of sending me to eat something, she mortified and humbled me exceedingly, saying that I was to wait and satisfy my hunger when the others went to the refectory· I then remained in peace in my suffering. At that time, however, I was not allowed to complete my penance by continuing to abstain from drinking ; but after having submitted to this prohibition, I was permitted to re-commence, and I then passed fifty days without taking anything to drink, and I did the same every Friday. I was always equally satisfied whether what I asked for was granted or refused ; it was sufficient for me to obey.

My persecutor did not cease to attack me in every way, with the exception of impurity, which had been forbidden him by my Divine Master. Nevertheless, he once caused me to suffer untold torture, in the following manner. One day my Superior said to me : " Go and

take the place of our King before the Blessed Sacrament."
When there, I felt so strongly assailed by the most
abominable temptation of impurity, that it seemed as
though I were already in hell. I en-
dured this suffering for several hours,
until my Superior relieved me from that
obedience, adding that I was no longer
to take the place of our King before
the Blessed Sacrament, but that of a
good religious of the Visitation.

89. She is assailed one day with a certain temptation while taking the place of the King before the Blessed Sacrament.

Thereupon all my torments immediately ceased, and I
found myself overwhelmed with consolation, during
which my Sovereign Lord gave me the following
instructions.

In the first place He wished me to be in a continual
state of sacrifice. To this end, He said He would increase
my sensitiveness and repugnance so
that I should not be able to do anything
except with difficulty and great effort.
This was in order to provide me with
matter for self-conquest, even in the most trivial and
indifferent things. I can attest that I have ever since
experienced this. He added that I should no longer
taste any sweetness, except in the bitterness of Calvary,
since He would make me find a martyrdom in all those
things in which others find joy, delight and temporal
happiness. It has pleased Him that I should experience
this in a very marked manner, since everything which
could be called pleasure has become a torment to me.
Even in the little recreations which are sometimes given,
my sufferings exceeded those of a violent fever; nevertheless He willed that I should in no way distinguish
myself from the others. This caused me to exclaim:

90. Everywhere she finds the bitter- ness of Calvary.

" O my Sovereign Good! how dearly have I to buy this pleasure! "

Such suffering awaited me in the refectory and in bed that the mere thought of going there drew from me sighs and tears; but my occupations and the parlour were altogether insufferable to me. I do not remember having gone to them except with repugnance, in order to conquer which, I was obliged to do extreme violence to myself, and this often caused me to kneel down and ask God for strength to overcome myself. Writing was not less painful to me, not so much because I did so kneeling as on account of other sufferings I felt when thus occupied.

Esteem, praise and applause pained me more than any humiliation, contempt and abjection could have pained the vainest and the most ambitious of honour. On such occasions I was wont to say: " O my God, let all the fury of hell be armed against me rather than that the tongues of creatures should utter empty praise, flattery or applause. Grant rather that I may be overwhelmed with every kind of humiliation, pain, contradiction and confusion! " He gave me an insatiable thirst for them, although, when the occasions presented themselves, He made me feel them so keenly that at times I could not help manifesting this exteriorly; yet I could not bear to see that I was so wanting in humility and mortification, as not to be able to suffer without its being perceived by others. My sole consolation was to have recourse to the love of my abjection, and thus thank my Sovereign Lord for making me appear such as I really was in order to annihilate me in the esteem of creatures.

Moreover, He willed that I should receive everything

as coming from Him without procuring anything for myself; that I should abandon all to Him without disposing of anything; and that I should thank Him for suffering as well as for enjoyment. On the most painful and humiliating occasions I should consider that I not only deserved these, but even greater ones, and should offer the pain I experienced for the persons who afflicted me. Further, I was always to speak of Him with great respect, of my neighbour with esteem and compassion, and of myself never, or, at least, briefly and with contempt, unless for His glory He should make me do otherwise. I was ever to attribute all the good and the glory to His sovereign Greatness, and all the evil to myself; never to seek consolation out of Him, and even when He granted it to me, to renounce and offer it to Him. I was to cling to nothing, to empty and despoil myself of everything, to love nothing but Him, in Him and for the love of Him, to see in all things naught but Him and the interests of His glory in complete forgetfulness of myself. And though I was to do all my actions for Him, He willed that His Divine Heart should have a special part in each one. For example, when at recreation, I was to offer Him Its share by enduring sufferings, humiliations, mortifications and the rest, with which He would always provide me, and which on that account I was to accept willingly. In like manner in the refectory I was to give up for Its satisfaction whatever was most to my taste, and so on with all my other exercises.

He likewise forbade me to judge, accuse or condemn anyone but myself. He gave me many other instructions, and as I was astonished at their number, He told me

91. Our Lord Wills that she should accept all as coming from Him and be occupied solely with Him.

to fear nothing, for He was a good Master, being as powerful to have His teaching carried into effect, as He was all-wise both to teach and to govern well. Thus I can affirm that, whether I would or not, I was obliged to do what He wished in spite of my natural repugnance.

Being before the Blessed Sacrament one day of Its octave, I received from my God signal tokens of His love, and felt urged with the desire **92. The great** of making Him some return, and of **revelation of the** rendering Him love for love. " Thou **devotion to the** canst not make Me a greater return of **Sacred Heart.** love," He said, " than by doing what I **(June, 1675.)** have so often asked of thee." Then, discovering to me His Divine Heart, He said : " Behold this Heart, Which has loved men so much, that It has spared nothing, even to exhausting and consuming Itself, in order to testify to them Its love ; and in return I receive from the greater number nothing but ingratitude by reason of their irreverence and sacrileges, and by the coldness and contempt which they show Me in this Sacrament of Love. But what I feel the most keenly is that it is hearts which are consecrated to Me, that treat Me thus. Therefore, I ask of thee that the Friday after the Octave of Corpus Christi be set apart for a special Feast to honour My Heart, by communicating on that day and making reparation to It by a solemn act, in order to make amends for the indignities which It has received during the time It has been exposed on the altars. I promise thee that My Heart shall expand Itself to shed in abundance the influence of Its divine love upon those who shall thus honour It, and cause It to be honoured." And when I replied that I knew not how to accomplish what He had so long desired of me, He told me to address myself to His servant, whom He had sent me for the accomplishment of this design. Having done this, he (Father de la Colombière) ordered me to commit to writing all that I had made known to him concerning the Sacred Heart of Jesus, as well as several other things which referred to It for the greater glory of God. This was a cause of great comfort to me, as this holy man not only taught me how to correspond to His designs, but also reassured me in the great fear I had of being deceived which was a constant trouble to me. And though it pleased Our Lord to withdraw him from this town and employ him for the conversion of heretics,[1] I received this blow with perfect submission to the Will of God, Who had allowed him to be of such use to me during the short time he had been here. When I ventured afterwards to reflect upon my loss, my Divine Master forthwith reproved me, saying : " What ! am I not sufficient for thee, I Who am thy beginning and thy last end ? " This sufficed to make me abandon all to Him, for I was convinced that He would not fail to provide me with everything that was necessary.

93. She is to address herself to Father de la Colombière for the accomplishment of this design.

As yet I had been unable to find means to begin the devotion to the Sacred Heart for which alone I lived. The first opportunity which His goodness afforded me occurred on the Feast of St. Margaret which, having fallen

94. The feast of St. Margaret, July 20th, 1685.

---

[1] The Rev. Fr. de la Colombière left Paray in 1676, being sent to England as Chaplain to Her Royal Highness, the Duchess of York, Marie Beatrice d'Este.

on a Friday, I asked our Sister Novices, of whom I
then had the charge, that, instead of giving me the
little marks of honour which they had intended to
offer me on my feast, they should pay them to the
Sacred Heart of Our Lord Jesus Christ. To this they
willingly agreed, arranging a little altar whereon they
placed a small ink etching representing
the Divine Heart. We then endea-
voured to pay It all the homage with
which It inspired us. This drew upon
me, and also upon them, many humilia-
tions and mortifications, for I was accused of wishing
to introduce a new devotion.

**95. The little feast
in the novitiate
gives rise to con-
tradictions.**

As for myself, these sufferings were a great consolation
to me, but I feared lest this Divine Heart should be dis-
honoured ; for all I heard was like so many swords which
transpierced my heart. I was forbidden henceforth to
put any picture of the Sacred Heart in a conspicuous
place, being allowed merely to honour It in private.[1]
In my affliction I knew not to whom to have recourse
except to Himself, Who always sustained my failing
courage, saying unceasingly to me : " Fear nothing, I shall
reign in spite of My enemies, and of all who oppose Me."
This consoled me greatly, for my one desire was to see
His reign established. I, therefore, abandoned to Him
the defence of His own cause whilst I suffered in silence.

**96. Persecution
on account of the
dismissal of Mlle.
de Chambron.**

Persecutions of various kinds arising at
that time, it seemed indeed as if all hell
were let loose against me, and that
everything conspired to annihilate me.
Nevertheless, I must own that never

[1] The Superior at that time was Mother Marie Christine Melun,
who governed the Monastery of Paray from 1684-1690.

did I experience greater interior peace and joy than when I was threatened with imprisonment and with being cited, even as my Good Master, before an earthly prince,[1] being moreover looked upon as a laughing-stock and a visionary whom imagination had made tenacious of her delusions.   I do not say this in order to make others believe I suffered much, but rather to manifest the great mercy of my God towards me, for I esteemed and cherished nothing so much as the share He gave me of His Cross, a most delicious viand of which I never grew weary.

If only I had been free to communicate often, I should have possessed all that my heart could wish.   Once when I ardently longed for Him, my Divine Master presented Himself to me when I was in the act of carrying away some sweepings and addressed me thus: " My daughter, I have heard thy sighs, and the desires of thy heart are so pleasing to Me, that if I had not instituted My Divine Sacrament of Love, I would do so now for thy sake in order to have the pleasure of dwelling in thy soul, and of taking My repose of love in thy heart."   This filled me with such intense ardour that I felt my soul, as it were, in a transport, and I could only exclaim: " O Love!   O! the excess of the love of a God towards so miserable a creature ! " Throughout my life, this has acted as a powerful incentive to enkindle within me feelings of gratitude towards this pure Love.

97. Her ardent desire for Holy Communion wins for her from Our Lord an incomparable answer which fills her with love and gratitude.

On one occasion when I was praying before the

[1] The Cardinal Prince de Bouillon, commendatory Abbot of Cluny, then residing at Paray.

Blessed Sacrament on the Feast of Corpus Christi, a person suddenly appeared before me all enveloped in flames, the heat of which penetrated me so powerfully that I believed myself to be burning as well.

98. She relieves the suffering soul of a Benedictine.

The pitiable condition in which I beheld him caused me to shed an abundance of tears. He told me that he was that Benedictine monk to whom I once went to Confession, and who had ordered me to receive Holy Communion, and that, as a reward for this, God had allowed him to have recourse to me that he might obtain some alleviation in his sufferings. He asked me to apply to his soul all that I should do and suffer for three months, which I promised with the consent of my Superiors. He then went on to say that the cause of his suffering was his preferring his own interests to the glory of God, through too great attachment to his own reputation ; secondly, a want of charity towards his brethren ; and finally, too natural an affection for creatures, many proofs of which he had manifested in his spiritual dealings with them, thereby greatly displeasing God.

But it would be difficult for me to express what I had to suffer during those three months. For he never left me, and on the side on which he stood, I seemed to be all on fire ; this caused me such intense suffering that my tears and groans were continual. My Superior, being moved with compassion, ordered me to perform severe penances, and in particular to take the discipline, because the bodily pains and sufferings, imposed upon me through charity, greatly relieved those which this Sanctity of love inflicted upon me as a slight sample of what It causes those poor souls to endure. At the end of three months he appeared to me in a very different state ; he was bathed in joy and glory, and about to be admitted into eternal bliss. He thanked me and promised to be my protector before God. I had fallen ill at the time, but as my suffering ceased with his, I soon recovered.

My Sovereign Lord also made known to me that, when He was about to abandon any of those souls for whom

99. Our Lord causes her to endure the anguish of a soul threatened with damnation. He wished me to suffer, He would place me in the state of a reprobate soul, making me feel the desolation in which it finds itself at the hour of death. I have never experienced anything more terrible and can find no words to describe it. Once when I was working alone, a religious who was still living was shown to me, and I distinctly heard the words : " Behold this nun who is one only in name ; I am on the point of rejecting her from My Heart and abandoning her to herself." At the same time I was seized with such great fear that, prostrating myself on the ground, I remained thus for some time wholly unable to recover. I forthwith offered myself to Divine Justice in order to suffer all that It should please, so that this soul might not be abandoned to itself. Thereupon it seemed as if His just anger were turned against me, for I was filled with terrible anguish and desolation, and I felt a crushing weight upon my shoulders. If I sought to raise my eyes, I beheld a God irritated against me and armed with rods and scourges which were ready to fall upon me. All within my soul appeared in a state of rebellion and confusion : my enemy attacked me on every side with violent temptations, especially with despair, and I sought to flee from Him Who pursued me, from Whose sight nevertheless I could not hide myself ;

in order to do so, there is no kind of torment I would
not have endured.   Moreover, I suffered dreadful confusion in thinking that my interior anguish was known
to everyone.   I could not even pray or express my
sufferings except by my tears, saying: "Ah! what a
terrible thing it is to fall into the hands of the living
God!"   At other times, prostrating myself with my
face to the ground, I said: "Strike, my God!   Cut,
burn and consume all that is displeasing to Thee,
spare neither my body, my life, my flesh, nor my
blood, provided that Thou save that soul for all
eternity."

I acknowledge that I could not long have endured so
painful a state, had not His loving mercy sustained me
beneath the rigour of His justice.   As it
**100.   She offers
herself to bear the
weight of the
Divine wrath in
the place of guilty
souls.**
was, I fell ill and had great difficulty in
recovering.   He often placed me in this
painful condition, and He once showed
me the chastisement He was about to
inflict on some souls; but I cast myself
at His Sacred Feet saying: "O my Saviour, I beseech Thee
rather to wreak Thy vengeance upon me and blot me
out of the Book of Life than to permit these souls which
have cost Thee so dear to perish!"   And He answered:
"But they love thee not and cease not to afflict thee."
"It matters not, my God, provided they love Thee, I
will not cease entreating Thee to pardon them."   "Let
Me do as I will, I can bear with them no longer."
Embracing Him still more closely, I replied: "No,
my Lord, I will not leave Thee till Thou hast pardoned them."   "I will do so," He said, "if thou
wilt be surety for them."   "Yes, my God, but I will
pay Thee only with Thy own goods, which are the

treasures of Thy Sacred Heart." Thereupon He was satisfied.

Another time, when the Sisters were working in common, picking hemp, I withdrew into a small courtyard, near the Blessed Sacrament, where, doing my work on my knees, I felt myself wholly rapt in interior and exterior recollection, and at the same time, the Adorable Heart of my Jesus appeared to me brighter than the sun. It was surrounded by the flames of Its pure love, and encircled by Seraphim, who sang in marvellous harmony: "Love triumphs, love enjoys, the love of the Sacred Heart rejoices!" These blessed spirits invited me to unite with them in praising this Divine Heart, but I did not dare do so. They reproved me, telling me they had come in order to form an association with me, whereby to render It a perpetual homage of love, adoration and praise, and that, for this purpose, they would take my place before the Blessed Sacrament. Thus I might be able, by their means, to love It continually, and, as they would participate in my love and suffer in my person, I, on my part, should rejoice in and with them. At the same time they wrote this association in the Sacred Heart in letters of gold, and in indelible characters of love. This lasted from two to three hours, and I have felt the effects thereof throughout my life, both by the assistance I received, and by the sweetness which it produced and continued to produce in me, although I felt overwhelmed with confusion. From that day I addressed them by no other name, when praying to them, than by that of my divine associates. This grace gave me so great a desire for purity of intention, and so high an idea of that which

101. The harmony of the Seraphim, her divine associates.

is necessary in order to converse with God, that nothing connected therewith appeared to me pure enough.

Once when one of our Sisters[1] was in a state of lethargy, so that there was no hope of giving her the last Sacraments, the community, and especially Our Mother,[2] were filled with grief. The latter, therefore, with a view to obtaining this grace, ordered me to promise Our Lord I would do whatever He would give me to understand was His desire. No sooner had I done so, than this Sovereign of my soul said that the Sister would not die without receiving the graces we rightly desired for her, provided that I promised Him three things, which He absolutely demanded of me. The first was, never to refuse any charge in religion; the second, not to refuse to go to the parlour; nor to write, which was the third demand. I confess that my whole being shuddered at this request, owing to the extreme repugnance and aversion which I felt, and I replied: "O my Lord, Thou dost indeed attack my weak points; nevertheless I will ask permission." This was immediately granted by my Superior in spite of my distress which I made no attempt to conceal from her. He then made me promise all in the form of a vow, that I might not be able to revoke it. But alas! how often have I been unfaithful to it, for He did not remove my aversion, which continued throughout my

102. She obtains by a painful sacrifice the grace of the last Sacraments for the little Sister de Senecé.

[1] It was a Sister of the "Little Habit," a privileged child called Antoinette Rosalie de Senecé. She had made the vow of chastity when seven years of age, and she was only thirteen when she died on April 26th, 1684, after having pronounced conditionally the three vows of religion.

[2] Mother Grefié.

life; the Sister, however, was able to receive the last Sacraments.

In order to show the extent of my infidelity in the midst of these great favours, I must say that, feeling once an ardent desire to make my annual Retreat, and wishing to prepare myself, I conceived the idea, some days beforehand, of engraving the Name of Jesus for a second time on my heart.[1] This, however, I did in such a manner that an open wound was formed. On the eve of my Retreat, I mentioned it to my Superior, who replied that she would have a remedy applied to prevent any serious consequences. This made me complain to Our Lord: "O my only Love! Wilt Thou permit others to see the wound I have inflicted on myself for the love of Thee? Art Thou not powerful enough to heal it, Thou Who art the Sovereign remedy of all my miseries?" Touched at length by the pain I felt in being obliged to make this known, He promised me that I should be cured by the morrow, and such was indeed the case. But not having seen Our Mother, I was unable to inform her of it, before receiving a note from her, in which she told me to show my wound to the bearer thereof,[2] who would apply the remedy.

103. The Holy Name of Jesus on her heart.

But, as it was healed, I believed myself dispensed from this obedience until I had spoken to Our Mother, to whom I went for the purpose of explaining that, as the wound was healed, I had not done what she had ordered in the note. My God! how great was the severity I met with for this want of ready obedience, not only from her,

---

[1] This was in autumn, 1679.
[2] This was Sister Marie Madeleine des Escures.

but also from my Sovereign Master. He kept me beneath His Sacred Feet for about five days, during which I could do nothing but weep over my disobedience and implore His forgiveness by continual penances. As for my Superior, she treated me on this occasion with pitiless severity, according as Our Lord inspired her, depriving me of Holy Communion which was the greatest torture I could have endured in this life, for I would rather a thousand times have been condemned to death. Moreover, she made me show the wound to the Sister, who, finding it healed, would not apply any remedy; nevertheless, I suffered great confusion.

But I considered all this as nothing, for there is no kind of torment which I would not have suffered, on account of the sorrow I felt at having displeased my Sovereign Lord. After having given me to understand how displeasing to Him is the least want of obedience in the soul of a religious, and having made me experience the penalty thereof, He Himself came to dry my tears and reanimate my soul during the last days of my retreat. But in spite of the greatness of His love my sufferings did not end there. The thought that I had displeased Him sufficed to make me melt into tears. For He gave me so clearly to [understand] what obedience is in the soul of a religious, that I own I had not realized it hitherto, but it would take too long to speak thereof. He told me that in punishment for my fault the Sacred Name, the engraving of which had cost me so much pain (in memory of that which He had endured when taking that Sacred Name), would no longer be visible, nor even the previous impressions which had hitherto appeared well-marked in different ways. I can truly say that my retreat was one of sorrow.

My infirmities were so continual that I was never well four days consecutively, and on one occasion my sufferings were so considerable that I was scarcely able to speak. That morning Our Mother came to me and gave me a note, saying that I was to do what was written therein, for she needed to be reassured as to whether what took place in me was the work of the Spirit of God. If such were the case, she required that He would restore me to perfect health for the space of five months, without its being necessary for me to take any remedy during that time. But if, on the contrary, it were the work of the evil spirit or of nature, she asked that I should remain in the same state in which I then was. It would be impossible to say how much this note made me suffer, the more so as what was contained therein had been revealed to me before I read it. I was then ordered to leave the Infirmary, and that with words inspired by Our Lord to render it more painful and mortifying to nature. Thereupon I presented the note to my Sovereign, Who well knew its contents. He replied : " I promise thee, My daughter, that as a proof of the good Spirit by Which thou art led, I would have given her as many years of health as she has asked months and even any other assurances she might have required." At the Elevation of the Blessed Sacrament I felt, in a most sensible manner, that all my infirmities were withdrawn, as though a garment had been taken off me. I forthwith enjoyed the health and strength of a most robust person who had not been ill for a long time. Thus I spent the

104. Mother Greyflé orders her to ask for five months of health, as a proof that it is truly the Spirit of God Which guides her.

time desired,[1] at the expiration of which I relapsed into
my former state.

At another time when I was suffering from fever, my
Superior ordered me to leave the Infirmary to go into
Retreat,[2] as it was my turn, saying to

105.   M o t h e r
Greflé makes her
leave the Infirmary
in spite of the fever
from which she is
suffering, in order
to send her into
retreat.   Our Lord
cures her.

me : " I commend you to the care of
Our Lord Jesus Christ. Let Him direct,
govern, and cure you according to His
Will."   Although I was a little surprised—for at the time I was shivering
with fever —I nevertheless withdrew to
obey the order given me. This I did
all the more joyfully, seeing myself
given up to the care of my good Master, and having the
opportunity of bearing something for the love of Him. It
was indifferent to me in what manner He would have me
make my retreat, whether in suffering or in enjoyment.
"All is well," I said to myself, " provided He is satisfied
and I love Him, that is enough for me."   But no sooner
had I shut myself up alone with Him, than He appeared
to me, as I lay prostrate on the ground, shivering with
cold and pain. He raised me up and loaded me with
caresses, saying : "At last thou art wholly Mine and
given up entirely to My care ; therefore I intend to
give thee back in perfect health to those who have thus
placed thee sick in My hands."   And He restored me so
completely that it seemed as though I had never been ill.
This astonished everyone, especially my Superior who
knew what had taken place.

[1] Viz., until December, 1683, for, at the end of the five months,
Mother Greyfié had ordered the Servant of God to ask that she
might remain in good health, " until the expiration of the year in
which this first obedience had been given her."
[2] In autumn, 1681.

I never spent a retreat in such joy and spiritual delight.
I seemed to be in heaven by reason of the great and
repeated favours lavished upon me
and the intimacy I enjoyed with my
Lord Jesus Christ, His most Holy
Mother, my good Angel Guardian and
my blessed Father St. Francis of Sales.
But I will not here specify in detail the
singular graces I received, for it would
take too long. I will only say that my
Divine Director, in order to console me
for the pain He had caused me in effacing His Sacred
and Adorable Name which, at the cost of so much
suffering, I had engraven on my heart, vouchsafed
Himself to imprint It interiorly and stamp It exteriorly with the seal and fire of His pure love. This
He did in a manner which filled me with more joy
and consolation than the former had caused me pain
and affliction.

**106. She experi-
ences exquisite joys
in this retreat and
exercises the great-
est rigour upon
herself. Our Lord
restrains her in the
excess of her
penances.**

But as nothing was wanting to me but the cross without which I could not live or take any pleasure, not even
heavenly and divine—since all my delight was to see
myself conformed to my suffering Jesus—I thought of
nothing but of treating my body with all the rigour that
the liberty which had been given me permitted. In truth,
I made my body experience this both as regards penances,
and food and sleep ; for I made myself a bed of potsherds
upon which I lay with great delight, although nature
shuddered, but in vain, for I did not listen to it. Once I
wanted to perform a certain act of penance, the austerity
of which greatly attracted me, for I thought I could
thereby revenge upon myself the insults which Our Lord
receives in the most Holy Sacrament from me, miserable

sinner that I am, as well as from all who dishonour Him therein. . . . But when I was about to put my plan into execution, my Sovereign Master forbade me, saying that He desired to restore me in perfect health to my Superior, who had confided and entrusted me to His care. He added that the sacrifice of my desire would be more agreeable to Him than the fulfilment of it, and that, being a Spirit, He desired also sacrifices of the spirit. Thereupon I remained content and submissive.

Once, as I was approaching the Holy Table, the Sacred Host appeared to me shining like the sun, the brilliancy of which was more than I could bear. **107. He places on her head a crown of thorns.** In the midst thereof I beheld Our Lord holding a crown of thorns which He placed upon my head shortly after I had received Him, saying at the same time : " Receive this crown, My daughter, as a sign of that which will soon be given thee in order to make thee conformable to Me." I did not then understand the meaning of these words, but the effects which followed made them clear to me. Shortly after I received two such terrible blows on the head, that ever since it seems to me as though the crown of my head were surrounded by sharp and painful thorns the pricks of which are to last to the end of my life. I give infinite thanks for it to my God Who grants such great graces to His miserable victim. But, alas ! as I often tell Him, victims should be innocent, and I am but a criminal. Nevertheless I acknowledge that I am more beholden to my Sovereign Lord for this precious crown of thorns than if He had made me a present of all the diadems of the greatest monarchs of the earth, the more so as no one can take it from me, and that happily it often obliges me to lie awake at night, and commune with the sole object of my love, for I find it impossible to rest my head on the bed, even as my good Master was unable to rest His Adorable Head on the Cross. It was a cause of inconceivable joy and consolation to me to see myself thus, in some measure, conformed to Him. He willed by means of this suffering, in union with the merits of His being crowned with thorns, that I should ask of God His Father, the conversion of sinners as also humility for those proud heads, whose haughtiness displeased Him so much and inflicted so great an injury on Him.

Another time during the carnival, that is to say about five weeks before Ash Wednesday, He appeared to me

108. She carries the cross with Our Lord and consents to be crucified by a severe illness. after Holy Communion under the figure of an ECCE HOMO laden with His Cross, covered with wounds and gashes, His Adorable Blood flowing on all sides. He said in a sorrowful voice full of anguish: " Is there no one to take pity on Me and share My sorrow in the pitiful state to which sinners reduce Me, especially at the present time?" Prostrating myself with tears and groans, at His Sacred Feet, I offered myself to Him, and taking on my shoulders that heavy cross, all studded with nails, I was overwhelmed with its weight. I then understood better the grievousness and malice of sin, for which I felt such a horror, that I would have preferred a thousand times to cast myself into hell than to commit a single one wilfully. " O accursed sin," I exclaimed, " how detestable thou art, since thou dost inflict such injury on my Sovereign Good ! " He then gave me to understand that it was not enough to carry the cross, but that I must fasten myself

to it with Him, in order to keep Him faithful company
by sharing in the sufferings, contempt, opprobrium and
other indignities of which He was the victim. I forthwith
abandoned myself to Him for all that He would desire
to do in me and with me, allowing myself to be fastened
to the cross according to His good pleasure. An illness
soon made me feel the sharp points of those nails with
which the cross was studded, for I became a prey to
acute sufferings, in which I met with no other compassion
than contempt and humiliations under circumstances
most trying to nature. But alas ! what could I suffer that
could equal the greatness of my crimes ! They continually keep me in an abyss of confusion, since the time that
my God showed me the horrible sight of a soul in mortal
sin, and the grievousness thereof, attacking, as it does,
a goodness infinitely loving and being such a great
insult to Him. This sight makes me suffer more
than anything else, and I would that I had begun
to suffer all the pains due to the sins which I have
committed, that they might serve me as a means of
protection and prevent me from committing fresh sins.
Truly, I would rather undergo any pain than have
been so miserable as to have fallen into sin, even
though I were assured that my God, in His infinite
mercy, would forgive me without delivering me up to
these sufferings.

These desires for suffering generally lasted the whole
time of the carnival until Ash Wednesday, when I seemed
to be reduced to the last extremity,
109. Her suffer- without being able to find any consola-
ings during the tion or relief which did not increase my
time of Carnival. sufferings. I then suddenly felt sufficient strength and vigour to fast during Lent. This my

Sovereign Lord always graciously enabled me to do, although at times I was overwhelmed with sufferings of all kinds. On commencing some exercise, I often felt as though it would be impossible for me to hold out to the end; nevertheless, I began the next with the same difficulty, saying: "O my God, grant me the grace to be able to continue to the end," and I returned thanks to my Sovereign Lord for thus measuring my minutes by the clock of His Passion so that all my hours might strike in unison with His sorrows.

When He intended to gratify me with some new cross, He prepared me for it by an abundance of favours and spiritual delights so great that, had they continued, it would have been impossible for me to bear them. At such times I exclaimed: "O my only Love, I sacrifice all these delights to Thee! Keep them for holy souls who will glorify Thee by them more than I do. I wish for Thee alone, bereft upon the Cross, where I desire to love Thee alone for the love of Thyself. O take all the rest from me, so that I may love Thee without admixture of pleasure or self-interest!" Then it was that, like a wise and experienced Director, He occasionally took pleasure in contradicting my wishes, making me enjoy when I would have wished to suffer. But I acknowledge that both one and the other came from Him, and that all the favours He has bestowed upon me proceeded purely from His mercy, for no creature ever resisted Him so much as I have done, not only by my infidelities, but also by the fear I had of being deceived. Hundreds of times I was astonished that He did not punish so much

110. Our Lord gives her occasionally spiritual delights, instead of the sufferings for which she begs.

resistance by casting me into an abyss and annihilating me.

Yet, however great my faults may be, that sole Love of my soul, in accordance with His Promise, never deprives me of His Divine Presence. But He makes it so terrible to me, when I have displeased Him, that there is no torment which would not be sweeter to me and to which I would not sacrifice myself a thousand times, rather than bear that Divine Presence and appear before the Sanctity of God with the least stain of sin on my soul. I would willingly have hidden myself at such times, and kept at a distance from Him, had I been able; but all my efforts were in vain, for I found everywhere that from which I fled, accompanied by torments so intense, that I seemed to be in purgatory. All within me suffered without any consolation or the desire of seeking any; thus, in the anguish of my heart, I sometimes exclaimed: "Oh! what a fearful thing it is to fall into the hands of a living God!" In this manner He purified me from my faults when I was not prompt and faithful enough to punish myself for them. Never indeed, did I receive any special graces from His goodness which were not preceded by this kind of torment; and after having received them, I felt, as it were, completely buried in a purgatory of humiliation and shame, in which my sufferings were beyond description. Nevertheless I always felt deep peace, and it seemed to me that nothing could disturb this peace of my heart, although the inferior part was often agitated, either by my passions or by my enemy. The latter, indeed, made every effort to this end, for he never has more power nor does he gain

111. The Divine Presence becomes very painful to her when she has in any way incurred His displeasure.

more advantage than over a soul in trouble and disquietude.[1]

Certified as true, this 22nd of July, 1715.

> (*Signed*):
> SISTER ANNE-ELISABETH DE LA GARDE.

> (*Signature of Registrar*):
> DOM DE BANSIÈRE,
> *Commissary.*
> CHALON.

Soon after the Beatification of the Servant of God the authenticity of this autograph manuscript was again attested by ecclesiastical authority in these words:

We, Apostolic Protonotary, Vicar General, Archdeacon of Autun, have recognized the biography written by herself, according to the orders of her Superiors, to be the autograph of Blessed Margaret Mary Alacoque, Virgin. It consists of sixty-four pages.

In testimony of which: Paray, February 26th, 1865.

> (*Signed*):
> G. BOUANGE, Apostolic Protonotary,
> *Vicar General, Archdeacon.*

Place of the seal of
Mgr. de Marguerye,
then Bishop of Autun.

---

[1] Here the Autobiography ends; for, as has been seen in the Preface to the French Edition of 1924, the Rev. Father Rolin, S.J., left Paray in the autumn of 1686, without having ordered Saint Margaret Mary to continue this memoir. The Saint, therefore, ceased to write; her holy death took place four years later, on October 17th, 1690.

CONCLUSION

As we close these pages, we recall the wish, so often expressed therein by Saint Margaret Mary, and the care she took, that their contents might never be brought to light.

But it did not enter into the designs of God to grant what the Saint, in her humility, so ardently desired. For the greater glory of the Sacred Heart the account of the divinely beautiful and familiar intercourse of Our Lord Jesus Christ with the chosen disciple of His Heart was to spread far and wide, so that many souls might be drawn to make Him " some return of love."

Actuated by the desire alone of procuring for the Divine Heart the love and reparation of countless souls, have we translated this autobiography.

God be praised !

PRAYERS

PRAYER OF ST. MARGARET MARY

My God, I offer Thee Thy well-beloved Son, in thanksgiving for all the benefits I have received from Thee. I offer Him as my adoration, my petition, my oblation and my resolutions; I offer Him as my love and my all. Receive, O Eternal Father, this offering for whatever Thou willest of me, since I have nothing to offer which is not unworthy of Thee, except Jesus, my Saviour, Whom Thou hast given me with so much love. Amen.

CONSECRATION
TO THE SACRED HEART OF JESUS
(Composed by St. Margaret Mary.)

O Sacred Heart of my Lord and Saviour Jesus Christ, to Thee I consecrate and offer up my person and my life, my actions, trials and sufferings, that my entire being may henceforth only be employed in loving, honoring and glorifying Thee. This is my irrevocable will, to belong entirely to Thee, and to do all for Thy love, renouncing with my whole heart all that can displease Thee.

I take Thee, O Sacred Heart, for the sole object of my love, the protection of my life, the pledge of my salvation, the remedy of my frailty and inconstancy, the reparation for all the defects of my life, and my secure refuge at the hour of my death. Be Thou, O most merciful Heart, my justification before God Thy Father, and screen me from His anger which I have so justly merited. I fear all from my own weakness and malice, but placing my entire confidence in Thee, O Heart of Love, I hope all from Thine infinite goodness. Annihilate in me all that can displease or resist Thee. Imprint Thy pure love so deeply in my heart that I may never forget Thee or be separated from Thee. I beseech Thee, through Thine infinite goodness, grant that my name be engraved on Thee, for in this I place all my happiness and all my glory, to live and to die as one of Thy devoted servants. Amen.

PRAYER TO ST. MARGARET MARY

O St. Margaret Mary, permitted by the Sacred Heart of Jesus to become partaker of Its divine treasures, obtain for us, we beseech thee, from that adorable Heart, the graces that we need. We ask for them with boundless confidence; may the divine Heart be willing to grant them to us through thy intercession, so that once again It may, through thee, be glorified and loved. Amen.

THIRTY-THREE VISITS TO
OUR LORD ON THE CROSS
(To be made on Fridays.)

Having read these pages, some souls may, perhaps, feel the desire of loving the Heart of Jesus more ardently, by living more in accordance with His life, and by praying for the conversion of sinners, this latter being one of the principal ends of the Devotion to the Sacred Heart.

There may also be souls who will be glad to know of an apostolate, hidden but real, taught by our Saviour Himself to St. Margaret Mary, with a view to the conversion of sinners, viz., Thirty-three Visits to our Lord on the Cross to be made on Fridays.

This is what the saint wrote about it: One Friday, during holy Mass, I felt a great desire to honor the sufferings of my crucified Spouse. He told me lovingly that He desired me, every Friday, to adore Him thirty-three times upon the Cross, the throne of His mercy. I was to prostrate myself humbly at His feet, and try to remain there in the dispositions of the Blessed Virgin during His Passion. I was to offer these acts of adoration to the Eternal Father together with the sufferings of her divine Son, to beg of Him the conversion of all hardened and faithless hearts who resist the impulse of His grace. He told me, moreover, that at the hour of death He will be favorable to those who have been faithful to this practice.

These thirty-three acts of adoration of our Lord on the Cross may be made anywhere on Fridays, and even while attending to one's ordinary work. They require no special attitude, formula or vocal prayer. A simple look of love and contrition, coming from the depths of our heart and sent up to our crucified Lord is sufficient to express our adoration and our gratitude to Him. It is also an appeal to the Blessed Virgin to intercede with the Heavenly Father for the conversion of sinners.

The efficacy of this devotion is proved by the consoling conversions which it obtains and by the holy deaths which are its fruit. We venture to say that it becomes a source of graces to all those who practice it, for never in vain does one approach Jesus Christ Crucified.

NOVENA IN HONOR OF
SAINT MARGARET MARY

This is a novena of mental prayer and pious practices, rather than of specific prayers in set formulas. We perform this novena in our mind and heart, by holy thoughts and affections, and by silent petitions in our own words—as well as by carrying out the pious practices indicated.

FIRST DAY

Let us honor Saint Margaret Mary today as *the privileged Child of the Blessed Virgin.* Jesus always loves to grant us His favors through Mary. We shall, therefore, entreat the saint to plead our cause with our heavenly Mother, so that we may more surely obtain the graces we ask through this novena.

Practice: *Purity of Intention.*

MAXIM OF THE SAINT

"One thing the Adorable Heart of Jesus asks of Its friends, viz., purity of intention, humility in action, and singleness of purpose." (ii, 481).

———

SECOND DAY

Let us honor Saint Margaret Mary today as *the beloved Disciple of the Heart of Jesus.* She ever allowed herself to be taught and formed by Him "after His own manner." Let us likewise place ourselves in those divine Hands, remembering what the saint said of Our Lord: "He told me that I had nothing to fear, because He was a good Master, as powerful to have His teaching carried into effect as He is learned in His doctrine and government." (ii, 103).

Practice: *Conformity to the Will of God.*

MAXIM OF THE SAINT

"Not only during prayer, but also at other times, keep yourself in the presence of Our Lord, as a disciple who is before his Master and anxious to learn to do His Will perfectly by giving up his own will." (ii, 707).

THIRD DAY

Let us honor Saint Margaret Mary today as *the Consoler of the Heart of Jesus.* One day Our Lord presented Himself to her as the "Ecce Homo," all torn and disfigured, saying: "I have found no one willing to offer Me a place of rest in this suffering and painful state."—"Thereupon I offered Him the *heart* He had given me that He might rest therein." (ii, 180-181). Can we not imitate our saint in this?

Practice: *To kiss the wounds of our crucifix in a spirit of true contrition.*

MAXIM OF THE SAINT

"In order to console my Jesus for the contempt, insults, sacrileges, profanations and other indignities heaped upon Him . . . I will neither complain nor excuse myself." (ii, 741).

FOURTH DAY

Let us honor Saint Margaret Mary today as *the Confidante of the Heart of Jesus.* Our Lord once said to her: "If thou art faithful to Me and followest Me, I will teach thee to know Me, and I will manifest Myself to thee." (ii, 47). It was because of her fidelity that He communicated Himself to her and revealed to her the incomprehensible secrets of His Adorable Heart.

Each time that we are faithful to grace, we incline the Holy Ghost to communicate Himself to us.

Practice: *To keep our sufferings a secret between God and ourselves.*

MAXIM OF THE SAINT

"To work and to suffer through love, and in silence, is indeed a secret known only to the lovers of the Well-Beloved." (ii, 403).

FIFTH DAY

Let us honor Saint Margaret Mary today as *the Victim of the Heart of Jesus,* and let us meditate on these words which Our Lord addressed to her: "My daughter, I come to thee as Sovereign Sacrificer." (ii, 90). She adds: "He wished me to be in a continual state of sacrifice." (ii, 101).

We are only able to follow the saint at a distance, but what need hinder us from striving to bring the spirit of sacrifice more fully into our lives?

Practice: *To accept all the trials that Providence sends us.*

MAXIM OF THE SAINT

"Let us then submit to the orders of our Sovereign Lord and, in spite of all that seems hard and painful, let us confess that He is good and just in all that He does, and that He deserves to be honored and loved at all times." (ii, 244).

SIXTH DAY

Let us honor Saint Margaret Mary today as *the Adorer of the Heart of Jesus.* Our saint was in a state of constant adoration, because she always kept herself annihilated through love and in love. Being favored with the sensible and habitual presence of her Lord and God, she kept, so to say, a feast of Perpetual Adoration in the depths of her *heart.*

If we cannot imitate such close attention to the divine presence, let us at least try, from time to time during the day, to offer to God acts of adoration which will glorify Him and put us in our real place as creatures before their Creator.

Practice: *When in the presence of the Blessed Sacrament, let us, by our humility and our fervor, be adorers "in spirit and in truth."*

MAXIM OF THE SAINT

"Our Lord wills that you should honor His life of consummation in the Blessed Sacrament. You must be like a lighted taper which has no other end than to be burnt away in His honor." (ii, 733).

SEVENTH DAY

Let us honor Saint Margaret Mary today as *the Instrument of the mercies of the Heart of Jesus.* One day Our Lord said to her: "I desire to make of thee a compound of My Love and of My Mercy." (ii, 46). Another time, referring to the graces with which He had loaded her, He said: "Thou must not keep these graces to thyself, nor be sparing in distributing them to others, for I have willed to use thy *heart* as a channel for conveying them into souls according to My designs; by this means many will be saved from the abyss of perdition." (ii, 35).

Let us, then, with entire confidence, have recourse to the saint, knowing that she has been commissioned by the Heart of Jesus to cause the waters of His divine mercy to flood our souls.

Practice: *To abandon ourselves to the merciful Providence of the Sacred Heart.*

MAXIM OF THE SAINT

"If you would put His benevolence under an obligation to take special care of you, abandon yourself entirely to His Adorable Heart, putting aside your own interests, in order to devote yourself wholeheartedly and lovingly to the work He has given you to do." (ii, 262).

EIGHTH DAY

Let us honor Saint Margaret Mary today as *the*

Heiress of the Treasures of the Heart of Jesus. It was He
Himself who conferred upon her this sublime and exceptional title with all its prerogatives, and He confirmed it in the following words: "As I have already
promised thee, thou shalt possess the treasures of My
Heart . . . and I will permit thee to distribute them as
thou wilt, in favor of souls that are ready to receive
them." (ii, 193-194).

Who would not wish to be among that privileged
number . . .? Let us, however, not forget that if we
would merit divine favors, we must prepare our souls
for them.

Practice: *Let us strive to cleanse our hearts so that they may
be ready to receive the outpourings of the Sacred Heart of
Jesus.*

MAXIM OF THE SAINT

"His love urges Him to distribute the inexhaustible
treasures of His sanctifying and salutary graces to
souls of good will. He seeks hearts that are empty, in
order to fill them with the sweet unction of His burning love." (ii, 532).

NINTH DAY

Let us honor Saint Margaret Mary today as *the Apostle of the Heart of Jesus.* To become an apostle a special
vocation and mission are needed. This was undoubt-
edly the case with our saint: Our Lord Himself called
her and deputed her for her mission.

He drew her close to His Divine Heart, and made
her rest within It; then, after having inflamed her with

the ardors of His love, He confided to her the mission of spreading the devotion to His Sacred Heart throughout the Church. Saint Margaret Mary spent herself in this saving work. Our Lord had said to her: "Fear nothing, I will reign in spite of My enemies and of all those who would oppose Me." (ii, 105). "Believest thou that I can do this? If thou dost believe it, thou shalt behold the power of My Heart in the magnificence of My love." (ii, 249).

The saint did believe, and Our Lord's words have been fulfilled: the reign of the Sacred Heart now extends to the ends of the world.

Practice: *To let no opportunity pass by of spreading the devotion to the Sacred Heart of Jesus.*

MAXIM OF THE SAINT

"He promises great rewards to those who work to extend His Kingdom." (ii, 530).

PRAYER

O Saint Margaret Mary! Thou whom the Sacred Heart of Jesus has made a participator of His divine treasures, we implore thee to obtain all the graces we stand in need of from that Adorable Heart. We ask them of Him with unlimited confidence. May the Divine Heart vouchsafe to grant them to us through thy intercession, so that He may yet again be glorified and loved through thee. Amen.

(The words of Our Lord which are quoted in this novena are excerpted from *Life and Writings of St. Margaret Mary.*)

LITANY OF THE
MOST SACRED HEART OF JESUS

(For public or private use.)

Lord, have mercy on us.
  Christ, have mercy on us.
Lord, have mercy on us. Christ, hear us.
  Christ, graciously hear us.
God the Father of Heaven,
  Have mercy on us.
God the Son, Redeemer of the world,
  Have mercy on us.
God the Holy Ghost,
  Have mercy on us.
Holy Trinity, One God,
  Have mercy on us.

Heart of Jesus, Son of the Eternal Father,
  Have mercy on us.
Heart of Jesus, formed by the Holy Ghost in the
  womb of the Virgin Mother,
  Have mercy on us.
Heart of Jesus, substantially united to the Word of
  God, *etc.*
Heart of Jesus, of infinite majesty,
Heart of Jesus, holy Temple of God,
Heart of Jesus, Tabernacle of the Most High,
Heart of Jesus, House of God and Gate of Heaven,
Heart of Jesus, burning Furnace of charity,
Heart of Jesus, Vessel of justice and love,
Heart of Jesus, full of goodness and love,
Heart of Jesus, Abyss of all virtues,
Heart of Jesus, most worthy of all praise,
Heart of Jesus, King and center of all hearts,

Heart of Jesus, in Whom are all the treasures of wisdom and knowledge,

Heart of Jesus, in Whom dwelleth all the fullness of the Divinity,

Heart of Jesus, in Whom the Father was well pleased,

Heart of Jesus, of Whose fullness we have all received,

Heart of Jesus, desire of the everlasting hills,

Heart of Jesus, patient and abounding in mercy,

Heart of Jesus, rich unto all who call upon Thee,

Heart of Jesus, Fountain of life and holiness,

Heart of Jesus, Propitiation for our sins,

Heart of Jesus, filled with reproaches,

Heart of Jesus, bruised for our offences,

Heart of Jesus, made obedient unto death,

Heart of Jesus, pierced with a lance,

Heart of Jesus, Source of all consolation,

Heart of Jesus, our Life and Resurrection,

Heart of Jesus, our Peace and Reconciliation,

Heart of Jesus, Victim for our sins,

Heart of Jesus, Salvation of those who hope in Thee,

Heart of Jesus, Hope of those who die in Thee,

Heart of Jesus, Delight of all the saints,

Lamb of God, Who takest away the sins of the world, *Spare us, O Lord.*

Lamb of God, Who takest away the sins of the world, *Graciously hear us, O Lord.*

Lamb of God, Who takest away the sins of the world, *Have mercy on us.*

V. Jesus meek and humble of heart,

R. *Make our hearts like unto Thine.*

Let Us Pray

Almighty and eternal God, consider the Heart of Thy well-beloved Son and the praises and satisfaction He offers Thee in the name of sinners; appeased by worthy homage, pardon those who implore Thy mercy, in the name of the same Jesus Christ Thy Son, Who lives and reigns with Thee, world without end. R. *Amen.*

LITANY IN HONOR OF
SAINT MARGARET MARY

(For private devotion only.)

Lord, have mercy on us.
   Christ, have mercy on us.
Lord, have mercy on us. Christ, hear us.
   Christ, graciously hear us.
God the Father of Heaven,
   Have mercy on us.
God the Son, Redeemer of the world,
   Have mercy on us.
God the Holy Ghost,
   Have mercy on us.
Holy Trinity, one God,
   Have mercy on us.

Holy Mary, Mother of God and Patroness of the Order of the Visitation, *pray for us.*
Saint Margaret Mary, disciple and apostle of the Heart of Jesus, *pray for us.*
Thou who didst have the Immaculate Virgin for thy Mother and Mistress, *etc.*

Precious pearl of the Kingdom of Heaven,

Thou who wast associated with the seraphim in
adoring the Heart of Jesus,

Victim and holocaust of the Heart of Jesus,

Privileged adorer of the Heart of Jesus,

Faithful image of the Heart of Jesus,

Thou who, like St. John, didst repose on the Heart
of Jesus,

Pure dove who didst make thy dwelling in the
opening of the Heart of Jesus,

Thou who didst live profoundly hidden in the Heart
of Jesus,

Model of obedience and mortification,

Faithful imitator of the meekness and humility of
the Heart of Jesus,

Violet of the garden of St. Francis de Sales who
didst shed throughout the Church the good odor
of Jesus Christ,

Thou who wast crucified with Christ,

Thou whom the Holy Ghost favored with the gift of
prophecy,

Most wise and gentle instructress of souls called to
the religious life,

Merciful advocate of sinners,

Charitable benefactress of the sick,

Joy of thy holy Order and glory of thy people,

Thou who dost extend thy special protection to all
who are devoted to the Heart of Jesus,

Lamb of God, Who takest away the sins of the
world, *Spare us, O Lord.*

Lamb of God, Who takest away the sins of the
world, *Graciously hear us, O Lord.*

Lamb of God, Who takest away the sins of the

world, *Have mercy on us.*

V. Grace is poured abroad on thy lips.
R. *Therefore God hath blessed thee forever.*

Let Us Pray

O Lord Jesus Christ, Who hast wonderfully revealed to Saint Margaret Mary the unfathomable riches of Thy Heart, grant that through her merits and following her example, we may love Thee in all things and above all things, and may thus be accounted worthy to obtain an eternal resting place in Thy Heart, Who livest and reignest with the Father and the Holy Ghost, world without end. R. *Amen.*

If you have enjoyed this book, consider making your next selection from among the following . . .

Raised from the Dead. Fr. Hebert 13.50
Autobiography of St. Margaret Mary 4.00
Thoughts and Sayings of St. Margaret Mary 3.00
The Voice of the Saints. Comp. by Francis Johnston 5.00
The 12 Steps to Holiness and Salvation. St. Alphonsus . . 6.00
The Rosary and the Crisis of Faith. Cirrincione/Nelson . . 1.25
Sin and Its Consequences. Cardinal Manning 5.00
Fourfold Sovereignty of God. Cardinal Manning 5.00
Catholic Apologetics Today. Fr. Most 8.00
Dialogue of St. Catherine of Siena. Transl. Thorold 9.00
Catholic Answer to Jehovah's Witnesses. D'Angelo 8.00
Twelve Promises of the Sacred Heart. (100 cards) 5.00
St. Aloysius Gonzaga. Fr. Meschler 10.00
The Love of Mary. D. Roberto 7.00
Begone Satan. Fr. Vogl 2.00
The Prophets and Our Times. Fr. R. G. Culleton 10.00
St. Therese, The Little Flower. John Beevers 4.50
Mary, The Second Eve. Cardinal Newman 2.50
Devotion to Infant Jesus of Prague. Booklet 75
The Faith of Our Fathers. Cardinal Gibbons 13.00
The Wonder of Guadalupe. Francis Johnston 6.00
Apologetics. Msgr. Paul Glenn 9.00
Baltimore Catechism No. 1 . . . . 3.00
Baltimore Catechism No. 2 . . . . 4.00
Baltimore Catechism No. 3 . . . . 7.00
An Explanation of the Baltimore Catechism. Kinkead . . . 13.00
Bible History. Schuster 10.00
Blessed Eucharist. Fr. Mueller 13.00
Catholic Catechism. Fr. Faerber 5.00
The Devil. Fr. Delaporte 5.00
Dogmatic Theology for the Laity. Fr. Premm 15.00
Evidence of Satan in the Modern World. Cristiani 8.50
Fifteen Promises of Mary. (100 cards) 5.00
Life of Anne Catherine Emmerich. 2 vols. Schmoger . . . 37.50
Life of the Blessed Virgin Mary. Emmerich 13.50
Prayer to St. Michael. (100 leaflets) 5.00
Prayerbook of Favorite Litanies. Fr. Hebert 8.50
Preparation for Death. (Abridged). St. Alphonsus 7.00
Purgatory Explained. Schouppe 12.50
Purgatory Explained. (pocket, unabr.). Schouppe 5.00
Spiritual Conferences. Tauler 10.00
Trustful Surrender to Divine Providence. Bl. Claude 4.00
Wife, Mother and Mystic. Bessieres 7.00
The Agony of Jesus. Padre Pio 1.00

At your bookdealer or direct from the publisher.

Prices guaranteed through December 31, 1992.